Off the Wall—Dive Tales

A WALL IS WHAT SCUBA DIVERS DIVE ON,
AND THE HUMOR IS A LITTLE OFF THE WALL

Sue Webb

PublishAmerica
Baltimore

First printing

PublishAmerica has allowed this work to remain exactly as the author intended, verbatim, without editorial input.

Back cover book synopsis by F.C. Blake

Hardcover 978-1-4626-2669-4
Softcover 978-1-4626-2670-0
PAperback 978-1-4626-4308-0
PUBLISHED BY PUBLISHAMERICA, LLLP
www.publishamerica.com
Baltimore

Printed in the United States of America

CONTENTS

ACKNOWLEDGMENTS

I'd like to thank all the dive shop owners, dive masters, and dive assistants who helped create the most memorable and fun times of my life. I'd like to thank all the pals, buddies and friends we made along the way; with whom we shared a dive, a laugh and a good time. I'd like to send a shout out to Ron Tinker, of Adventure Sports, Gresham, Oregon who taught us to dive and began our journey. Like also to especially thank Neil Mitchell of Aitutaki Scuba for his hospitality and friendship. Hiriam, Wani and all the guys at the former Rainbow Reef Divers of Tavenui, Fiji—thanks for memories.

Thanks to Phyllis Kent, my younger sister, who made me realize I had interesting stories to tell. Thanks to Pamela Cheney, my older sister, who told me I had writing talent that should be developed.

Colossal thanks to Florence Calderone Blake, I couldn't have written this book without her. Also thanks to David Smigelski, Mail Tribune, Medford, Oregon; Dan McFarland, Central Point Journal and Rogue Valley Times, Central Point, Oregon and Kevin Widdison, The Daily Courier, Grants Pass, Oregon for publishing excerpts to keep me encouraged.

And finally, thanks to Russ; my buddy, partner, husband and friend who came to my rescue many times, and kept me alive long enough to share our adventures.

INTRODUCTION

In the sixth grade a teacher gave me a book, *I Married Adventure*. I can still visualize it, a tattered clothbound book, the cardboard corners bent and frayed, imprinted with a zebra print grayed by a patina. It made a lasting impression.

A short time later, barely old enough to know the meaning of the word desperation, I heard an adult say, "Most people lead a life of quiet desperation." I decided, not me.

Years later I had an epiphany; it occurred suddenly like an exploding volcano. I knew what I wanted in life, to be Jimmy Buffett. I had to live a life of adventure.

I became a certified scuba diver and the adventure began. Being a diver opened a door of opportunity unlike anything I could have imagined, a life of incredible ups and downs. I've traveled the globe and glimpsed fascinating people and beautiful places.

Each journey began with knowledge. Dive travel in the early '90's required trudging to the library to peruse travel books. Later, with Internet access, the information became a click away. I utilized two basic sources: guidebooks and later tourism websites.

Research completed, if we decided to go, we began packing. Divers need their stuff and lots of it; we didn't however, need to take the cat. Fuzzy always knew when we were going on a trip. As soon as we took out a suitcase, he would climb in as if to say, "Can't I go too?" Fuzzy had to be removed multiple times during the arduous task.

Packing involved two oversized black hard-sided pieces of luggage, squeaking in under the length and width restrictions. We crammed them full of snorkels, fins, masks, buoyancy control devices, regulators and other necessary scuba gear. If we packed just right, one of us could sit on the top, while the other snapped the latch shut. Off we went.

The travel constituted the adventure, but the whole process—from pre-trip planning and anticipation, to our return and sharing our stories with friends and co-workers—made for an on-going fun and exciting run.

This book is a historical snapshot. The information was accurate at the time of our journeys. Since our travels occurred over a twenty year period, some things may have changed.

We explored the Pacific Northwest, Hawaii, Canada and Mexico with The Bottom Timers Dive Club of Vancouver, Washington. We traveled with members of the Oregon Society of Conchologists to Fiji. Australia, the Caribbean, South Pacific, and Micronesia were solo international trips. The book is chronological and may reflect some of these affiliations.

It's been a wonderful life. I invite you to take the cat out of the suitcase and come enjoy the adventures and antics with me.

CHAPTER 1

Entering Neptune's Realm

After an exhaustive search, he still couldn't find it.

"Find what?

"Dive shop."

"Why do you want to find a dive shop?"

"So we can learn to scuba dive."

My husband Russ' original career goal of marine biologist became sidetracked when he became a cellular technician. Regardless, his interest in the world's oceans, coral reefs and sea creatures remained. My interest in water went no further than a swimming pool on a hot day. A land-lubber native Oregonian, I became queasy at the sight of the sea.

"It'll be a great way to explore the world," he said. "We could travel, adventure, and sightsee on land and underwater." I must have been shortsighted; the steps into the pool represented my only underwater immersions.

I found myself thumbing through the yellow pages for a dive shop. Once we located one, we signed up, and jumped in.

After eight hours of work, we trudged to lecture. Following it, we dove into the pool to demonstrate our mastery, or lack of it. We rolled home after midnight.

Despite the long days, I enjoyed it. Our scuba instructor, Ron proved fun- loving, helpful and supportive. I'd taken Red Cross swim lessons, but barely passed pollywog. My confidence level equaled a polar bear on ice skates. I felt overwhelmed at first, almost flunking snorkel clearing; but thanks to the superhuman efforts of Ron, I slowly gained confidence.

We graduated from mask, snorkel and fins to BCs (buoyancy control devices) and regulators. Our class bobbed up and down like apples attempting to master buoyancy control. Tadpoles practiced putting on and taking off gear underwater. Buddies breathed through their partners' regulator. Hours flew by as we performed the same tasks. I spent more time than most, okay anybody, perfecting the skills.

We eventually mastered the necessary techniques to advance. Our first open water experience awaited us. The thought of leaving the pool frightened me, but the time had arrived to practice in the real world.

Our destination—a large mud puddle dubbed Klineline Lake, a residential pond stocked each spring with rainbow trout, so kids could snag one on opening day. It didn't exactly replicate the deep-sea experience, but it would do.

We arrived early in the morning fully outfitted, except for the fins I forgot. I borrowed a set, and then pulled on my dark wetsuit. I tied my hair back and put on my mask. The fins fit loosely, so I had to walk in an exaggerated manner to keep them on. The green aluminum cylinder proved an awkward fit. Since I'm short, the tank pushed my head forward.

"You look like a Ninja turtle," one of the kids with fishing poles observed.

"Do not. I'm not green."

"What are you guys doing?"

I had difficultly seeing him. My mask fogged up. "We're going scuba diving."

He began laughing.

We walked backwards, toward the water to avoid tripping over our fins. The kid enjoyed this; he laughed louder. We descended to escape the sound of his mirth.

After a few days' practice, check out time arrived. Ron observed us and ensured we'd demonstrated advancement skills. Russ and I could continue to Open Water I status. If successful, we'd be certified divers.

Sunrise Hotel, a well worn hostelry snuggled up to Washington's Hood Canal. Here we would be put to the final test. The inn lay just outside of Hoodsport, a quaint town that slept until spring, when awaken by tourists. Teeming with diners, ice cream and kite shops, bookstores and gas stations, it met the needs and supplied recreation for tourists.

Certification time arrived. We gathered our gear and went to the dock. I felt frightened, no terrified. I visualized an inspiration poster, SUCCESS. *I can do this*, I thought, *maybe*.

I watched as the first diver, selected by the instructor, because no one volunteered, leapt off the dock. He hit the water and went into hysteria. He flailed about, waving his arms and gasping for air. Ron joined him. He grabbed the piling and they descended into the depths.

With Ron's assistance he performed the perfunctory duties. The newbie boosted himself up the steps. He looked down; his wetsuit had been shredded by barnacles, as he grasped the piling on the descent. His face turned scarlet. I visualized another accomplishment placard.

Ron called the next diver. It wasn't me because one of the advantages of being short is there are a lot of people I can hide behind. One at a time, they jumped in. Russ breezed through it, "Showoff," I said. Then the attention turned to me. I remained the last unproven diver.

"I'm ready," I lied, and took a giant step off the dock. I didn't look; I wasn't the kind to look before I leaped. I hit the water. "Whoa," I said, trying to catch my breath, "It's freezing." Icy cold liquid slapped me in the face then worked its way into my wetsuit. All my senses were assaulted. I remained in a state of shock, but completed the necessary tasks. I climbed up the steps, but I felt so jubilant I could have flown.

Ron called us all together. We felt a huge sense of accomplishment. Wide smiles and hugs transferred among us, as we congratulated one another. A celebratory mood reigned, when Ron said, "Oh, by the way, there is one more thing." The mood changed; it grew quiet.

"Oh, what's that?" someone asked. "We thought we'd earned our C (certification) cards."

"You have to swallow a raw oyster."

"A what?" I asked.

"In order to be a real diver, you must swallow a raw oyster."

I gagged. The thought of slimy raw oysters made me nauseated. I didn't like the way they looked, or smelled or felt. "We'll have a ceremony tonight before dinner. You guys will swallow your oysters and I will present you with your C cards."

Ron doled the slime blobs out, one to each diver, with a napkin. "Okay, I'm going to recite a saying and when I'm done, everyone has to swallow their oyster," Ron said. "Over the lips and over the gums, look out stomach, here it comes."

I looked around, everyone did it, and so I did it. I began to gag. I spit it into the napkin.

Ron laughed. "That's good enough. Now you've had a taste of what it is to be a diver," he said.

Mission accomplished. My buddy and I attained the rank of certified divers. Let the adventures begin.

Ron, Russ, Sue and fellow newbies swallowing oysters at scuba certification. Hoodsport, Washington

CHAPTER 2

Cozumel: A Broad Monkeying Around

"...anyway, we were at about sixty feet down on Paradise Reef, when…" I was interrupted.

"Wait a minute. Paradise Reef in Cozumel?" a fellow diver asked. He looked at me as if I suffered from nitrogen narcosis.

"That's the one."

"The Mexican government razed that reef twenty years ago when they built the new International Pier."

"Yes, I know." What I didn't know at the time—we dove history.

"Not many divers had a chance to dive it. Could you tell me about it?"

"I will as best I can remember." I began to relate my story.

It constituted our first international trip. For me, a small town girl that led a sheltered life in Eastern Oregon, it proved an overwhelming experience. I grew up believing a river divided every state. I knew Washington lay on the other side of the Columbia. The thought of what might lie across the ocean represented a concept too immense for me to grasp.

We arrived at Cozumel when it offered raw adventure. Atlantis

Submarines hadn't launched yet. There weren't any Glass Bottom Boats in sight. Adventure Park didn't exist. Zip lining had yet to make its debut. Diving provided one of the few recreational pursuits.

A utilitarian stucco beach shack stood on the lonely shore. Attached to the front of it, a white board scrawled on with black and red house paint stated, "Here is what we offer you. The fastest boats around. Full Service 7:30A.M. to 7:30P.M. Boat Dive Departures 8:30A.M. - 12:30P.M. 1 P.M. - 5P.M."

Several tall, cylindrical-shaped cardboard bins stuffed with beach umbrellas and rolled-up beach mats, sat nearby. A large trough-like tub filled with water, held an assortment of masks, snorkels, and fins.

We approached the high counter. A Casablanca-like fan rattled overhead. It seemed more noisy than effective. A high-spirited young hombre greeted us. He sported only a pair of swim trunks, a smile, and his Mayan heritage.

"*Hola, amigos,*" he said. "You want to go diving today? We have fast boats."

"Yes, we would like to," Russ said.

"We can arrange that amigo," he continued. "And, how would you like to come to a very special fiesta later?" He held up a battered photo album, supporting it against his chest. Buxom barely-dressed women burst from its pages.

As he displayed the party book, I noticed that all the fingers were missing from his right hand.

"No, I don't think he'd be interested in that," I said before Russ had a chance to respond. The dive hawker saw me glance at his hand.

"*El Tiburon.* Shark," he said.

"Shark?" I repeated. My discomfort dissolved. Dread replaced it. None in my hometown wheat community had digits pre-empted by a sea creature.

Leery but undaunted, we rented tanks to make a shore dive. We chose the sunken airplane that lay just off the pier, behind the La

Ceiba Hotel.

The two-hundred-foot visibility dive proved disappointing. There wasn't much to see. We traded tanks and tried another shore dive off the old International Pier.

"Y'all ever been to Cousin Mel's before?" asked a lanky diver with a Texan drawl, as we turned on our tanks' air.

"Nope," I said, grabbing my mask and fins. *Funny he should ask,* I thought. Ironically, I had a Cousin Mel.

I almost expected our diving companion, to jump in with cowboy boots instead of dive boots, and a silver-buckled belt instead of a weight belt.

As it turned out, a number of our dive buddies on this trip would be Texans. Not surprising considering the close proximity. We'd find out in later travels that divers tended to choose destinations closest to home.

We fought the current to about forty-feet, our maximum depth. A rather unspectacular sandy bottom harboring a few crab and eels awaited us. I had scads of fun though.

My first warm water dive made me ecstatic. Without the onus of a quarter-inch wetsuit and a heavy weight belt to sink it, I felt free. I reveled in the marvel of being neutrally buoyant, basically weightless, without cumbersome restrictions on my movement. I experienced unfettered joy, jubilance.

Like a seal at Sea World anticipating its sardines, I performed loop-de-loops, somersaults, twists and twirls. I did it once, and then I did it again. I noticed the Lone Star State's diver watching me. I guess I provided more entertainment than the eels.

The dive's shallow depth gave me lots of time to play.

Almost an hour later, we surfaced and returned to the pier. The Texan popped up and swam in behind me.

As we kicked on our backs, he caught up to me. "Honey child," he said, "You looked like you were having the bass durn time. I hain't never seen somebody have so much fun!"

"I pretended to be an astronaut in outer space," I said. I felt the need to explain my exuberant behavior. I just had a blast.

We found a cozy café and had dinner, washed down with a Corona. I don't remember what we ate—probably some kind of fresh seafood—but it tasted great. Something about diving made most things taste delicious, with few exceptions.

We made four more dives: Paradise Reef, Gorgonian Flats, Chankanab Reef and Palancar Reef. Of the four dives, the now non-existent Paradise Reef proved our favorite.

Paradise Reef, a pleasant drift dive, served as home to an abundance of fish. The healthy reef extended down to a sandy bottom. Our timing proved fortuitous. It met its demise shortly after our visit, an unfortunate victim of the new pier.

Sea wasps lived and prospered on Chankanab Reef. They welcomed us in a painful, prickly manner. The few fish in the area had been lured by cold freshwater. It made the site hazy, compromising visibility of the sparse items of interest. "Not a great place to dive," Russ noted in his log. That summed it up.

Palancar Reef, where we descended to a depth of eighty-feet, offered an interactive opportunity. A slight current allowed us to slowly float by a variety of sea life. At forty feet, coral buttresses and stunning caves provided a pleasant diversion. Russ and I played tag swimming around, in and through the structures—they created a fun playground.

Gorgorian Flats, the site of the day's last dive, provided underwater awe. Two-hundred-foot visibility reigned, healthy life flourished. Surfing the current we glided by coral, sponges, and eels. A couple of our favorite fish, puffers and parrot fish, made an appearance. Conch and star shells lay scattered on the unspoiled sandy bottom.

We wanted to get out, quite literally, and see the island while we had the chance. Russ rented a Mexican VW bug. Cozumel could be toured in a day, due to its small size. The island revealed itself as an idyllic tropical paradise. White sand beaches fringed a jungle-like interior.

Thirsty, Russ pulled off the narrow road for an ice-cold beer; it never tasted better than in a red-hot place. The beach vendor's *palapa*—a post set in the sand covered by overlapping palm frond thatching—offered not only refreshment, but more, a monkey. The small fellow darted about atop the bar as if he were inspecting glasses. Did they remain filled, or did patrons need seconds?

"Dos Coronas por favor," I said. I'd been studying conversational Spanish for several weeks prior to our departure. I thought about asking for a *Dos Equis,* but *Dos, Dos Equis* sounded like I stuttered.

"Two beers coming right up," the barkeep replied in perfect English.

"Is that your monkey?" I asked. "He's really cute."

"No, he is my helper," he said. "I like little monkey around. You like monkey around?"

"Um, at the right time with the right person," I said. I began picking up on a theme here, "*If it happens in Cozumel, it stays in Cozumel,*" I thought.

Russ and I lingered for awhile to enjoy our beers and the sidekick's antics, and then continued on our way.

The following day we dove Yucab Reef and Los Glorious. They created memories for different reasons. One dive remained unforgettable because of humor; the other dive became indelible due to pain.

Yucab Reef, a favorite site teeming with schools of barracuda and sting rays, offered an unexpected surprise.

As I swam along at eighty-feet, enjoying the sights in front of me, I sensed something beside me. I turned my head, assuming it was Russ. It wasn't Russ, but rather a three-hundred pound grouper. Boy, did I do a double take. I looked the other direction. Russell lingered watching my reaction. He began laughing so explosively, his bubbles obscured my view of him.

At first I felt frightened, as the gigantic saltwater marine creature glided beside me, but then I thought, *This is kind of cool. I'll pretend like I'm in a huge aquarium.*

The grouper stayed for several minutes, then pulled in front of me, and swam off. I'm glad he joined me for awhile. He made a good buddy.

Our last dive, Los Glorious, proved anything but. Russell's tooth began aching. That ended our diving on Cozumel.

A couple of vacation days remained, so we flew to Chitzen Itza—on mainland Mexico—the Yucatan destination featured Mayan ruins. "Sounds interesting. I recall studying Mayans, Aztecs and Incas in sixth grade. I'd like go," I said.

Although interesting, not a sensible idea. The pressure changes in the small prop plane made Russ' toothache worse. "How's the tooth now?" I asked.

"Not too bad." Which I knew meant not too good. He's a stoic guy.

The Mexican army met us at the airport, attired in dark green and black splotched army fatigues. Diminutive men, wielding machine guns with bullets strapped diagonally across their chests, they reminded me of G.I. Joe action figures.

The ruins were federal property. We figured that explained the militia's presence. Not wishing to find out otherwise, we promptly hailed one of the waiting taxis.

A bucket of bolts Dodge Dart served as our transportation to the ruins. It had no back seat. We sat on a too-brightly colored, striped blanket on the floor. The loco taxi driver screamed across the jungle, in the tropical heat, to our destination. Maybe he thought the faster he went, the better the four-window air conditioning system worked. His speed had the cab's dingle-balls dancing like Wham-O high bouncers in a lottery selection machine. How the Virgin Mary managed to not fly off the dash, I'm not sure. The rosary, he had looped around the rear-view mirror, took a real beating.

It didn't take us long to get there.

The ruins boggled our minds. What the ancient civilization of Mayans had achieved, struck me as impressive beyond belief. The sprawling complex, a hub for their culture, had facilities for housing, recreation, worship and other daily activities such as bathing. Huge stone structures, beautifully constructed, rose with grandeur, some towering high into the sky.

El Castillo resembled the Egyptian pyramids. It lay at the center of the complex dominating the landscape. A step pyramid, the Mayans used it as timekeeping device.

El Caracol, a magnificent domed building, housed an early observatory.

The Great Ball Court served a doozy. A sculptured, paneled wall displayed the fate of a loser—a decapitated head. Ancient Mayans practiced human sacrifice. Afraid of spying further such representations, I avoided sightseeing and walked the grounds with Russ.

"Hey, how's the tooth doing?" I asked, as we boarded the flight back to Cozumel. *Maybe if I sound chipper, it'll cheer him up,* I thought.

He didn't answer. He just hung his head and held his hand over his cheek.

As soon as we landed, I hailed a taxi. "*Dentista.*" Luckily, it was a Spanish class word. The taxi driver dropped us off at an austere two-story, stucco building. He had taken us to the only available doctor—a gynecologist.

Russ pointed at his cheek to indicate he suffered from a toothache; it wasn't a word I'd learned in class.

The doctor wrote a prescription and gave us directions to the *farmacia*.

A man sporting a white doctor's coat stood behind the counter. To the rear of him, dingy bottles and dispensers, sat atop dusty glass shelves. Russ handed him the RX scribbled on a piece of notepad. The pharmacist smiled and nodded he understood.

He then walked to the back wall. After perusing his massive selection, he picked a compact white aerosol can off the shelf. He carried it back to the counter and set it directly in front of Russ. It read, Mr. Stud.

Russ tried to explain the problem existed in his mouth, not elsewhere. The prescription turned out to be for Novocaine.

Russ took a shot and we headed back to the hotel. We dug some aspirin out of the toiletries case, he took several, and we went to bed early.

"Suzy. Suzy," he moaned at midnight. "My tooth hurts."

Not knowing what to do, I called a taxi to return us to the gynecologist. Because the medical office also served as his dwelling, I assumed he'd be there.

We arrived back. I stood and banged on the door. Eventually the bleary-eyed doctor came to our rescue. I explained Russ remained in grief.

"I'll tell you what," he said. "I will call my friend who is a dentist. He is moving to Mexico City in the morning, but hasn't left yet," our medical miracle worker said.

Three long hours later, the dentist and his wife arrived. Mr. Stud hadn't yielded the desired results.

The dentist took a look, the verdict: abscess. So, at 3 A.M. on that sleepy Mexican morning, we crowded into the gynecologist's car, and went to the relocating dentist's office. Russ had his tooth pulled. "I feel much better."

We expressed our sincere gratitude to everyone for helping us.

What a relief. Our scheduled flight home—two hours away. The pressure changes would have made flying impossible.

"Wow, that's quite a story," my fellow diver said. "Now, what did I ask you again?"

"About diving in Cozumel before the International Pier construction decimated Paradise Reef. That's only one tale, I have many more."

"Well, tell me another."

"Okay, I will. I enjoy sharing my adventures. I truly do."

CHAPTER 3

Just Enjoy! On Holiday in British Columbia

Should we stuff the turkey and ourselves, over the long Thanksgiving holiday or wander out in the autumn chill in search of adventure? We chose the latter, but where? We studied the atlas in search of a place within a day's drive, where we could go diving.

Vancouver Island, B.C., rumored to be some of the best diving on the West Coast, caught our eye. Algae blooms decreased in winter. The improved visibility made even better diving.

We drove to Port Angeles, Washington and caught Black Ball's COHO ferry. The cruise-ship size transport featured gift shops and a cafeteria. It crossed the Strait of Juan de Fuca to Victoria, B.C. at the tip of Vancouver Island. A lovely town, steeped in as much British tradition as their tea, greeted passengers.

It seemed as though we'd made a transatlantic crossing, not merely sailed across the strait. The British flag unfurled over the skyline dominated by regal architecture. Locals spoke with an unmistakable accent. The newspapers heralded the latest escapades of Queen Elizabeth II and her heirs. United Kingdom's Royal Coat of Arms decorated the local square.

"It's like we're in England." I couldn't believe this international community thrived above the same Washington coast where I'd lived inland for many years. "It's a small world."

"I'd say we should get out more," Russ said, then added, "but I don't think that would be possible."

Exploring the waterfront, we found ourselves surrounded by friendly blokes out for a morning stroll. The Parliament Building, which featured a larger-than-life bronze statue of Queen Victoria, added an impressive highlight. The Empress Hotel, a regal four-hundred-sixty room vision of grandeur, built in Edwardian style over one-hundred years ago, sat along side.

"Let's stop for high tea," I suggested.

"Only one problem, that's in the afternoon, it's the wrong time of day."

"Right-o, Russell," I felt Victoria's influence. "Well cheerios and pip-pip then. We'll go to a tea shoppe and have a spot there."

We ambled around town. The English flavor intensified with a stop at Murchie's Tea & Coffee, "A Tradition of Elegance" since 1894. A tantalizing brew of teas, coffees and sweets blended together to create a delightful rise-and-shine aroma. The on-site bakery's staff stirred in the heavenly scents of cinnamon, cloves and a rack full of other spices.

"Everything smells yummy." I stopped to try and untangle the tantalizing mix. "Cinnamon rolls. They're making my mouth water."

"And, what would you like today?" the salesclerk asked. "The sticky buns are poppin' fresh."

"Well, I'd like one of everything, but I'll settle for a sticky bun and English Breakfast Tea, milk and sugar, please."

"I'll second that," Russ said.

Goodies in hand, we continued our walk. Nibbling our rolls and sipping our tea, we stopped to window shop. An age-old bookstore yielded reading material and advice on where to later lunch. The proprietor suggested, in a heavy brogue, "... at Bounces, heh, down the street, then around the alley to the left."

Russ and I browsed the shoppes until we got hungry, and then sought out Bounces. I tried asking several passersby; no luck. An amiable-looking older gentleman provided the answer. He removed his houndstooth cap, scratched his head, chuckled, and then said, "Ooh, Troy's at Trounces Alley. Just down to the alley, then left, heh?" We'd been walking around in circles and had passed it several times.

At Troy's, a mannequin dressed like a proper English lady, holding the British flag and a sign heralding, "Last Outpost of the British Empire" invited us in. A genteel waiter showed us to a table. "I'm gonna get the fish 'n chips," I said to Russ. "Maybe they'll come wrapped in newspaper. I haven't read today's yet."

"I realized something." My light bulb often lit on the obvious that just hadn't occurred to me yet. "These guys call French fries, chips."

"Not much gets by you, Suzy." Russ said, then yawned. He'd been the victim of many of my daffy insights. To me, they were nirvana.

The flaky and juicy beer-battered halibut, served with malt vinegar, proved delectable—although only served in tissue paper newsprint. The authentic atmosphere more than made up for the lack of the daily news. A small telly that sat elevated on a shelf by the bar, compensated by droning the local news and weather.

The weather forecaster announced, "Eight high, low three today in the Victoria area. For tomorrow, expect rain in the morning, possible clearing in the afternoon." The people exuded warmth, but Mother Nature didn't.

"Whoa, we can't go diving. We'll be human icicles. It didn't feel that bad."

"Easy, Suzy," Russ reminded me, "those are Celsius degrees, not Fahrenheit."

"Is it always this cold?" I'd asked a young fellow as we left the pub.

"No, not at all," he said with a grin, "sometimes, it's colder."

We camped out, sporting every layer of clothing I packed. Russ and I rattled around Rathtrevor Beach Provincial Park mostly by ourselves. It must have been the time of year; it appeared to be a premier destination. Old growth Douglas fir trees nestled up to a wide sandy beach overlooking an expansive sea.

"I can't believe we didn't need reservations to stay here."

"In the summer, I'm sure you would." Russ confirmed my impression.

The easily accessible waterfront park appeared well maintained. We found it interesting that only eight percent of tourists arrived from the Northwestern United States, thirteen percent came from neighboring Alberta, with the balance being local residents. "I guess we're not the only country with spectacular parks. I bet that eight percent would balloon, if people realized how beautiful our neighbor to the north is," I noted.

We followed British Columbia 1, a section of the Trans-Canada Highway, from Victoria along the coast. Open wooded areas allowed beach access. In rural areas, few lights existed. Dark skies and quiet nights created a lonely feeling in the isolated areas near the Campbell River, which lay above the 49th parallel.

Bald eagles and Canadian geese seemed to be common sights. Divers and sunbathers appeared uncommon sights.

We made two dives and found each location different. The first dive, at Rock Bay—north of the Campbell River—we found unexciting, not much color or life. The most interesting aspect may have been how the mollusks differed from those in the San Juans and Puget Sound of Washington. Far fewer shells seemed to exist in the area, a short distance north.

We then turned around and headed south. A dive equal to any we'd see on the coast of North America awaited us. The fantastic visibility for a cold water dive, at least 50 feet, rivaled the best of the San Juans in Washington or Channel Islands in California. Sea life embraced the site. A variety of mollusks populated the bottom. Fish skittered about and a wolf eel slithered around the bright red, orange, yellow and green neighborhood created by the kelp, anemones and sponges. Thirty-five-feet seemed to harbor the greatest diversity of underwater flora and fauna.

"I know why everything wants to live shallow. It's chilly down there," I said after we exited the water. Even with my new dry suit—that I couldn't have made the dive without—cold defined the experience. Russ never froze like I did. Guys seemed to deal with the extreme temperature better. This might explain why only a handful of women dove in cold water.

"Suzy, even if you want to, you can't keep adding air. One of these days you're going to end up on the surface with your feet over your head." Russ admonished me.

Russ had an uncanny ability to foretell future occurrences. "I sure hope not. That could be a dangerous stunt; and if any Bottom Timers (dive club members) saw it, I could end up with the Fin Flopper Award." It represented the dreadful, disputable honor for the dumbest trick anyone pulled the entire year.

I enjoyed the diving, thanks to our new dry suits. "Let's come back this summer, when the weather's warmer," I suggested. We did, and guess what?

A quick stop for a snack, and then we began our long drive home. As the grocer rang up our treats, he added with a smile, "Just enjoy."

Thank you. We did, and began planning that next fateful journey—with the Bottom Timers as witnesses.

CHAPTER 4

Big Island- Romp in King Kamehameha's Domain

A mammoth green sea turtle whooshed by me. With a single strong stroke of his flippers, he pulled away. Executing several more powerful pulls, he rose to the surface for a gulp of air, and then descended.

I imitated his stroke and continued swimming. He slowed down and waited for me. He glanced toward me, then swam alongside in the crystal-clear blue water. After awhile, he headed out to sea. Before he left, he reached forward with a flipper as if to scratch his head. Did he wonder if I might be coming along?

I found myself scratching my head too. Did we go to Kona, Hawaii and take the Bottom Timers Dive Club along with us? Yes, indeed. The entire group converged on the Big Island.

Our first destination would be Place of Refuge, (*Pu'uhonua o Hanaunau*). The national park offered magnificent diving. It remained open for evening use.

"Let's do a night dive," a club member suggested.

I'll give it a try, I thought. I tried it, briefly. The dark night and black water cast an ominous shadow over the experience. I found it creepy—more macabre creatures abounded than characters in a Tim Burton film. Shrimp inspired fear. Piercing, tiny red eyes peered out of the darkness. Ghostly creatures, scary and strange, lurked about. Devilish-looking creations leered out of crevices.

"Eek! I'm never doing that again," I said, fleeing the water. I logged my first, and last, night dive.

The Kona Coast wasn't a place for beachcombers. Few beaches existed. Black lava rock fringed the shores, replacing the white sand that uninitiated tourists may have come in search of. Fingers of volcanic basalt, once molten lava, protruded into the ocean. They provided the base for the reef that surrounded the island.

This dramatic, sculptured archipelago proved as perfect a magical kingdom for the Bottom Timers, as it had for ancient Hawaiian royalty.

We couldn't wait to go outside and play. Each morning we located our matching rental cars. After selecting the correct one, we'd head out to go diving.

First stop, Kona Coast Diver's to exchange our tanks. Vinny, a long time club member, needed to use the facilities. He went to the back of the building where two doors confronted him. He grabbed a door knob, about to enter, but stopped. He noticed an oval sign, Radio Room. He paused for a moment, and then stepped sideways to read the other door, Computer Room.

"Which is the men's room?" he asked. His need to know seemed somewhat urgent.

"The one with the seat that's up," the dive shop owner said, as he walked by carrying a scuba tank across the parking lot.

Missions accomplished, we hit the road. *Kihei*, aka Yellow Fishes, would be our destination on this day. There, nature had created the perfect set up for a dive. *Pahoehoe*—shiny, smooth lava with a ropy surface—served as an ideal staging ground. The *pahoehoe* provided a good place to lounge, and prepare for the dive. A gentle trade wind and balmy eighty-degrees added to the perfection, as everyone donned their gear and set up their tanks.

Suited up, we headed toward the end of the lava flow. Madame Pele—Goddess of Fire—accommodated us once again. The lava dropped off toward the sea in a gradual manner creating a virtual set of steps into the sea.

On the bottom step, we plopped down and put on our flippers. Fins on, we fell forward into the water. Yellow Hawaiian Tangs surrounded us like curious kids. We snorkeled out to a sufficient depth, and descended.

The reef appeared light-colored, but not as a result of coral bleaching. Healthy, it provided a home to a variety of fish. The predatory crown of thorn starfish population however, looked menacing.

At ninety-feet, the coral reef ended. Mollusks decorated the sandy bottom with sand trails. At the end of each path, a lump protruded. Under the sand, beautiful orange miters with ecru dots, and striking ivory augers with brown spots dwelled.

A little deeper, hundreds of sand eels swayed in the current, their movement created a hypnotic effect.

Bottom time expired quickly at this depth. Each of us began our ascent, following the reef back up. After a five minute safety stop we resurfaced, and snorkeled back in.

Getting out, proved much more difficult than getting in. The tide had gone out, lowering the water level. Climbing up on the bottom step proved challenging. The gentle trade wind had become a breezy, annoying blow that whooped up the surge.

Each diver struggled, trying to time the wave intervals, factoring in the surge, to return to our perch. All of us had to make several attempts, but eventually we found ourselves safely back on top of the rocks.

The club made several more dives, thankful they weren't quite as exciting.

On our last night, the Bottom Timers gathered to share what we deemed a special memory.

Trudy recalled the dive she made with Jerry and Vinny. Jerry's tank strap came loose. His tank floated above his back. When she glanced at Vinny, he laughed so hard, he had to hold his face mask on.

Jerry recalled the evening the club went to see hula dancers at a Polynesian show. Vinny pulled his chair out, and faced it toward the stage for a better view, so he had his back to the table. Over the course of the evening, all of us took our umbrellas out of their tropical drinks. We then quietly slipped them, one at a time, into his glass.

At first he didn't notice, his focus directed on the hula girls. Soon, he needed to push the toothpick shades aside with his straw, to be able to take a sip. Still, his center of attention remained the performers. He failed to look at his drink as the bumbershoots filled the glass. Eventually when he lifted his glass to take a sip, they all came tumbling out. "What the hey?" he said as he wiped at his shirt with a napkin. He finally caught on.

We all had a good laugh over that.

I asked Vinny about his most memorable moment. "I guess, swimming with the turtles," he said. He seemed non-committal. He may have had too many to choose from.

"I'll never forget the grass eels that stood on end at about 120 feet," Russ said. "They swayed back and forth like charmed snakes." He added, "I liked the hula dancers too."

I noticed. His focus on them didn't stop at the stories they told with their hands.

"I found the diving memorable, but man, you couldn't beat that the helicopter tour of the island," Todd said. "And the fact I went on a manta ray dive, but didn't see a manta ray."

"The other morning in the hotel room," Rich said, but would not elaborate further.

Captain Rick of Kona Coast Divers also had a memory to share. "I'll never forget the Bottom Timers. I've never had to fill so many tanks in my life!" He then added, "A real pleasure having all of you here."

Last and probably least, I shared my most memorable moment. It occurred on a sandy shore dive, when attempting to enter the water. I failed to read a wave correctly.

SMACK! the wave hit me. I got bashed. I flailed about on the shore like a beached whale. Diving in warm water, I wasn't wearing a wetsuit. Every cranny of my body filled with sand. Russell found this hilarious; he had just warned me to wait for the next set of waves. I had calmly reassured him I knew it would be okay.

I had sand in my pants. The bottom of my swimsuit sagged like a little kid's dirty diaper. Madame Peles' fury had nothing on me. The harder Russ laughed, the madder I got. I had to get in the water to cool off my hot head.

To my dismay, as I related my story, everyone laughed. I realized it probably was as funny as Russ thought. Maybe I'd think so later.

We finished off the evening in a jocular mood tinged with nostalgia.

The last morning on the island, we gathered for an early breakfast and quick meeting.

Russ, the club's president, called the meeting to order. "Well, I think we can all agree we've had a great time," he said. "Does anyone have anything they'd like to add?"

"The club would like to make two special presentations," Trudy said. "Our first is to Todd. We wanted to make sure you saw a manta ray," she said as she walked to Todd's table to hand him the plastic toy.

She returned to her table and picked up an ABC Stores bag.

"Last night at the Polynesian show, we noticed Sue became a tad jealous of the hula dancers," Trudy said.

"Here you go Sue, you can grab Russ' attention too," Trudy said as she handed me the bag.

I opened it. Inside, wrapped in cellophane, lay a polished coconut shell bra and a long grass-green hula shirt.

"Put it on!" Russ said.

"Maybe later," I said, thinking, *This could be fun.*

The time to depart the Big Island arrived. We drove past the *pahoehoe* fields to the Kailua-Kona airport. Words created from white pieces of coral lay on the black smooth lava, adding interest to the otherwise bleak scenery. Hearts with the names of lovers, like those carved into a tree, cluttered the roadside. *MAHALO*, a Hawaiian word meaning thanks, happened to be the last word we saw.

Mahalo for the memories Kona—had a marvelous time. Although sad to leave, Russ and I knew more good times lay ahead. I couldn't wait to see what hatched.

CHAPTER 5

Taking the Unforgettable Caribbean by Storm

"So many choices, which ones should we choose?" I asked Russ. We sat huddled over the world map, examining the Caribbean Sea archipelagos that stretched over a million square miles. The islands began south of Florida and ended off the coast of Venezuela.

The possibilities seemed overwhelming. I had difficulty deciding what flavor yogurt to buy. Furthermore, due to historical influences, the islands varied in language, culture, and ambience. Some shared the tropical climate and little else.

From the 16th century to the early 19th century, European powers fought for control of the archipelagos. Danes, Dutch, English, French, Irish, Spanish and Swedes left their imprints behind.

"If we choose our islands carefully, this could be like a European vacation," I surmised. A prolonged discussion followed. A less ambitious itinerary was agreed upon, with certain nonnegotiable terms.

"Have to go to one of the French West Indies." I'd long been enthralled by the language, cuisine, and the French people's style. Russ became acquainted with a citizen of Martinique through correspondence. He'd invited us to visit. Neither of us spoke French, which should make it more of an adventure.

Puerto Rico served as gateway to the Caribbean. From there American Eagle's turboprop aircraft whir across the ocean to other islands. The American territory failed to capture our imagination. We didn't make plans to stay, just stopover.

St. Kitts—the Mother Colony of the West Indies—Nevis, her smaller sister island, and Martinique would be our destinations. Nevis lay across a channel only a couple of miles away, as the crow flies. We found later, crows are wise to fly.

"Where are we?" I asked, rubbing my eyes. We awoke to the sound of the sea lapping on the shore. Russ and I remained groggy from twenty-hours of flight and few hours of sleep. Sunshine streaming in the window bought us back to life.

"St. Kitts."

"Oh, that's right. I forgot."

After crawling out of bed and grabbing a rejuvenating shower, we wandered out to explore the countryside.

A mother hen, her chicks, two sheep and a goat, accompanied us on our stroll down the gravel road.

The aroma of freshly baked bread permeated the air. We followed our noses to the Fancy Loaf Bakery. A friendly islander emerged from the one-room, brightly colored, stucco enterprise, which sat overlooking the sea. He yelled something in a language we didn't understand. He stopped for a moment, as if he were thinking, then said, "Morning, morning," and flashed a broad smile.

After a quick snack, we made arrangements to catch a ferry to Nevis. Our accommodations and diving reservations were there. A taxi delivered us to the dock terminal. What awaited us proved astounding.

The Charlestown, Nevis and St. Kitts ferry, might best be described as a cross between transportation and a circus, resplendent with side shows. The boat ran twice daily, with no Sunday service.

"Bet they need a day of rest, I'm surprised they don't take two. It looks like we're going for a ride, on a floating zoo," I said, then laughed at my unintentional poetry. It seemed an apt ode to the bizarre scene that unfolded before us.

Saturday, many of the residents of Nevis, took the ferryboat to St. Kitts to go shopping. Because of the need to move goods from the larger island to the smaller, the vessel also served as a freighter. As luck mandated, it was Saturday.

Passengers, of various sizes and descriptions, crowded the narrow pier. They jockeyed for position to secure passage for themselves and their treasures on the antiquated transport.

An elderly woman, clad in a faded duster of tropical flora, a hat crocheted in reggae colors, nylons rolled at the knee and running shoes, maneuvered through the crowd.

She advanced past women laden with groceries; beyond a middle-aged man with several rolls of galvanized fencing; by an older man with a caged chicken; and a young man with dreadlocks, who held a blaring boom box on his shoulder.

Her advancement showed considerable expertise. She wielded a pair of stacked Queen Anne dining chairs.

A mind-boggling spectacle surrounded us. Russ and I stood on the packed-to-the-gills cacophonous pier watching the frenetic activity our five, over-sized, burdensome pieces of luggage in tow. I realized that a simple, "Excuse me," would not suffice to board. We considered our options.

"Maybe we can find someone to help us," I suggested.

Without guidance, we might not make if off St. Kitts. We'd become acquainted with one person on the island—our taxi driver. As Russ watched the luggage, I searched for the driver. Luckily he hadn't left yet and I found him.

"May I ask a favor of you?" Do you think you could help us get aboard?" He stood there and considered my request briefly.

"I think I can do that."

The driver and I made our way back to Russ and the luggage. Because of what appeared to be the cabbie's connections with an unofficial longshoreman's group, we were hustled onto the ferry.

"Good thinking, Suzy."

"Every once in awhile I try to use the old bean."

The ferry, already packed with people, made us feel like sardines stuffed in an overfilled can. As we shuffled the narrow aisle, the temperature soared to over one-hundred degrees. Unsavory odors, like old gym socks, hung in the air.

"Now I know why travelers are willing to pay $100, to charter a small plane to make the two-mile crossing," I said.

Nevis turned out to be a charming little island, much quieter than St. Kitts.

After a brief taxi tour, we checked into a cozy, pink, beach-front cottage. The luggage stowed away, Russ and I were off to Noel's Auto Garage Service Center for a rental vehicle.

Russ made a stop at the local police station to obtain a Federation of St. Christopher & Nevis driver's permit. The licenser reminded us to drive on the left-hand side and that we should be aware of donkeys. "Donkeys?" I wondered.

"Yes, donkeys. Especially at night. They can come out of nowhere."

Russ pulled into Noel's, a family-owned business that operated out of a garage. A two-year-old wearing only a huge smile toddled around the car. He grabbed me by the finger and led me to the front door. Nailed on it—a printed sign:

GREAT MINDS DISCUSS IDEAS

GOOD MINDS DISCUSS THOUGHTS

SMALL MINDS DISCUSS PEOPLE

As I stood there and pondered how gems of knowledge can appear at anyplace at anytime, my thoughts were interrupted. "Please come in. I'm Noel's wife," the genial woman said.

She removed a calico cat, who vocalized its displeasure, from its comfortable napping spot on top of the ledger. The Mrs. then converted the rental rate from E.C. (Eastern Caribbean) to U.S. currency. After filling out a simple one-page rental agreement we were ready to go.

As we departed, Noel reached into the rented Samurai, winked, smiled and then stuck a KEEP LEFT decal on the inside of the window.

The small islet had only one dive shop, which operated out of the hotel. A short amble across a groomed tropical garden led to the dock, where the first stage water transportation floated. We loaded our gear onto the rowboat, to get to the larger boat farther out in the harbor.

Barely underway we spotted a hulking sailboat sitting atop a capsized twenty-foot boat. A small inflatable with two, distraught, muscular Nevisians aboard added to the chaotic scene.

A mass of confusion followed. The captain attempted to render aid, but it proved impossible. The men in the raft set off in pursuit of several red gas cans that bobbed in the open ocean like ping-pong balls. The sailors shouted back and forth at each other in several languages.

"Do you have a coast guard you could radio?" Russ asked

"Yes, but they're not that reliable. It's the French, you see. They don't know how to sail. See that boat?" The skipper pointed toward the shore to a massive sailboat that had run aground. "The French wrecked that boat there not long ago," he said, then sighed.

"I guess an occasional run-in is inevitable," I said. People come from all over the world to sail these waters. The flags of multiple countries flapped like colorful kites in the tropical breeze. The array of sailing vessels that glided by resembled an international parade.

Resigning ourselves to the fact we could do nothing to help; the captain tied a buoy to the boat and watched it disappear into the deep. He then backed away and we continued on our way.

"Exciting day so far. Wonder what might happen next." I'd soon find out.

By the time we arrived at the dive site, the seas had turned against us. Large swells rocked the boat in an unsteady fashion. Divers awkwardly attempted to suit up. They struggled to maintain their balance while being thrown forwards then backwards.

Queasiness began to take hold. Russ and I tried to keep our footing. After a concerted effort, we were able to pull on our fins. One giant step off the back of the boat yielded immediate relief.

The peaceful descent in crystal-clear, eighty-degree water provided us with more than one-hundred-foot visibility. Calm transcended on us as we floated toward the bottom. Regulators echoing our breathing interrupted the silence.

The dive master led us on a coral garden tour. Our group kicked past an overhang. Small beady eyes and feelers peered out at us.

Stingrays lay low, jetting in and out of the swaying soft coral. Multitudes of pint-size, neon fish gathered around us. Entranced in the beauty of our surroundings, I felt immersed in nature. Much too soon we needed to ascend.

The dive master gave the thumbs up signal. Everyone headed for the surface.

The seas had grown angrier. We swam to the back of the boat, fighting the swells. I grabbed the ladder. As I attempted to climb aboard, a huge wave clobbered me. The collapsible ladder swung back smashing my legs. I held on until the next set of waves passed. Exhausted, I used my remaining strength to hoist myself aboard.

"What a relief it is," I said to Russell, as he followed behind me. The feeling of ease didn't last long. Nausea replaced it. I knew as soon as we were underway, I would be okay—except, the boat wouldn't start. The dive master hammered on the engine as I hung over the side. The smell of gasoline and oil fueled my seasickness.

Finally the craft sparked, coughed, chugged, then reluctantly kicked over. As we glided across the water I started feeling better—never felt so good to feel normal.

Other dives on Nevis proved enjoyable, not quite as unforgettable.

"Think we've had our share of memorable experiences." I suggested we charter a fishing boat to return to St. Kitts.

Our final destination, Martinique, sat relatively close to St. Kitts; however we had to return to Puerto Rico, then turn around and fly back. "Too bad we used frequent flyer miles for this trip," I said. "We could have earned a bunch."

Martinique resembled France plopped in the Caribbean Sea. Exciting and happening, loud and fast—a sharp contrast from the proper, quiet, English Nevis.

It fascinated me, how the islands so close in proximity, could have developed so differently. Our friend, Marcel, told us, "I feel more kinship with France, than with my neighboring Caribbean islands."

"Perhaps because the adjacent isles don't appreciate their sailing skills," I whispered to Russ.

Martinique's largest city is Fort-de-France; the population exceeds one-hundred-thousand. Residents for the most part, seem to enjoy a comfortable standard of living.

Our introduction to the island—a chauffeured Mercedes from the airport—served as a striking contrast to our ferry boat ride to Nevis. I liked this better.

Communicating proved our greatest challenge. Few spoke English. We came to realize the value of conveying information with facial expressions, hand signals, and body language. The French, a lively animated bunch, mastered it.

Fun resulted from trying to figure things out. To successfully complete everyday tasks entertained us.

A parking meter we encountered became one of our first quandaries. It proved more complex than a run-of-the-mill American meter. Francs, we knew, were the local currency (pre-Euros.) We had some. What we didn't understand: Why every time we inserted a small coin into the intimidating looking meter, it dropped into the change basket, kerpluck.

The complex meter had a place to insert coins, plus several, serious-looking red buttons, a meter and an annulation dial.

"What's annulation?" I wondered.

"I dunno, but it must be an important step in the process," Russ conjectured.

We tried various combinations of coin, annulation and red buttons several times, the only result being a loud thud.

I noted a tourist's bureau across the street. I sauntered over, hoping someone might speak English. Exactly one person did.

"Uh, we're…" I cleared my throat, feeling a little foolish. "We're, uh, having a little bit of trouble getting the parking meter to work." I showed her the coins we tried using.

She listened in bemusement then politely explained the small coin represented a larger denomination—too much for the meter to accept.

If we'd just applied logic, we wouldn't have figured it out either.

Some things we figured out. I had the most luck with name brands that were imported to the States. I knew what the products were. Yoplait, I learned resulted in yogurt. French fries and French bread didn't work—too generic. We ended up eating a lot of yogurt, not many potatoes or much bread.

Eating, at times, left us in a pickle. One day at the beach we neglected to eat lunch. French restaurants don't open until late for dinner; there isn't much available late in the afternoon.

We managed to find a beach snack shack—no English spoken. The maitre d' seated us and, with a flourish, presented us with menus. Russ and I stared at them 'til our eyes crossed. I closed them and chose.

The waiter showed up. I pointed to the unknown quantity. He looked at Russ. Russ shook his head up and down, and then held up two fingers. "Be interesting to see what we're having for lunch," I commented.

The server arrived with two dry chicken sandwiches. It occurred to me they would be better with mustard. An idea suddenly came to me,

"Do you have any Grey Poupon?" His face lit up and off he went. He returned with the mustard.

Feeling proud of ourselves, we took the plunge and tried to find a dive shop.

Russ and I wandered the wharf, the center of tourist activities. Russ spotted a large catamaran with scuba tanks. Next to it sat a sandwich sign, *PLONGEE*. Our ship had come in.

The French dive boat might best be described as a place where nothing goes on—or at least, not much. The cruise to the dive site included complimentary Litl' Punch—that packed a big wallop—and being buzzed by an aircraft.

The diving proved divine and the dive master a devilish delight. Jacques, a handsome Frenchman, had fun teasing me with an eel. He wanted me to touch it. I didn't want to. He took his regulator out, bit my finger, then shook his head no—indicating it wouldn't bite. Jacques took another breath, removed his breathing apparatus again, and proceeded to suck my finger.

Now, at this point I wasn't thinking about the eel, but I still had no intention of feeling it. He pulled me down to the bottom where the cage sat. When he let go of me, to get the elongated fish, I made my getaway. I laughed so hard bubbles flew like a champagne bottle that just got uncorked. Jacques did too.

Russ and I never travel without learning something new. On this trip I learned it's unnecessary to speak the same language to communicate—humor is universal. I learned that gems of knowledge can occur in the most unlikely places. And finally I learned, if you ever want mustard, ask for Grey Poupon. That will cut it.

CHAPTER 6

Baja La Bamba Ramblings

Four *amigos*, we stumbled along, singing loud and off key. Jerry and Trudy, Russ and I, arm-in-arm ambled wobbly-legged out of the hotel lobby. Slightly tipsy from our potent welcome drinks, but frisky from our trip to the spa, we decided to walk to town. We crossed a stone lane. "Do you guys know what this road is made of?" I asked.

"Nooo," my three friends replied.

"Cabostones." Laughter rang out. I thought, *This is going to be a fun trip.*

Ambling alongside the oceanfront, we stopped by the cruise ship dock. It hummed with activity. Souvenir-hawker's booths, brimming with trinkets of various sizes and descriptions crowded the available space. Raucous noise rang out. "For you, best price," promised one vendor after the next, as they aggressively pushed their wares.

Passenger boats brought tourists, prosperity and the American work ethic to Cabo San Lucas. One merchant told us, "I am tired. When the cruise ships come in, I work from five in the morning until five a night."

He showed us his schedule. On some days, two luxury liners appeared. Each day a vessel anchored, merchants had to rise early to display their wares. At night, everything needed to be packed up: ironwood dolphins, chess sets, silver jewelry, Cabo t-shirts, oversize *sombreros*, and woven blankets.

The next day, sellers, tireless and dedicated, returned to repeat the process.

Not all visitors arrived via cruise ship. Many flew in, and stayed at luxury resorts that offered modern amenities. Cabo's retailers had an instinct for what American tourists wanted, and provided it. If visitors desired a burger, pizza, or ice cream—fast food chains provided a taste of home. But, Baja California Sur offered much more.

The Mexican tourist bureau enticed us to—"Feel the Warmth." It wasn't just how it felt, but how it seduced the senses. *Mariachis* strolling in an open air *cantina*; spicy food igniting appetites; a wisp of a brown-eyed girl, imploring the purchase of *chicle*; vibrant-colored, stucco *haciendas* baking in the sun—all contributed to the magic.

"All things are possible in Mexico," our waiter responded one morning, after we'd asked if we could have some toast. My entourage soon believed him.

We acquired a taste for the place. Huge platters of fresh seafood: lobster, shrimp and squid abounded for a pittance. Free-flowing tequila washed down the sea's harvest. Good food and friends fueled an ongoing *fiesta*.

Since we were on vacation, Russ, our friends and I, indulged ourselves. We didn't realize to what degree, until we ran into a young couple we'd met in Cabo at La Paz. "Oh, look!" one of our new friends exclaimed, "It's the tequila people."

Ostensibly, we had come to go diving. Leaving Cabo behind, we rented a couple of misfit cars, then headed north on the costal highway.

We made a stop, en route to La Paz, at Chileno Beach. The picturesque, white-sand shore provided water sport enthusiasts with a variety of options. A beach shack's owner rented snorkeling accessories and scuba tanks. Russ and Jerry secured gear. Each of us outfitted ourselves, then we hotfooted it across the warm sand to the water.

We scampered past palm trees and bright, oversized, striped beach umbrellas. Sun lovers lazed underneath, rubbing sunscreen on each other's backs. Dodging kids engaged in horseplay; we entered the gentle surf, to a reef-less environs.

One dive down, we tried another. Both shore dives were neither remarkable nor memorable, but pleasurable experiences. Chileno proved a great place to lounge on the beach and relax.

Continuing north along the coast, we stopped to snorkel at Playa Santa Maria. The underwater scenery again failed to mesmerize. No tourist services awaited. However, the protected, horseshoe-shaped bay provided a nice spot for a swim.

The four *amigos* pushed on.

Our destination for the evening, La Paz, came into view. At the entry to the city we encountered a massive white stucco "thing." What could it be?

After a lively debate, we narrowed it down to a whale's tail or a dove. After all, the dove represented peace, and La Paz means "the peace" in Spanish. Try to argue this point with three friends—who all happen to be divers. It could be nothing other than a whale's tail.

Controversy continued to rage, until one evening when shopping, we asked a *senorita* staffing a *tienda*. Good-natured and helpful, she—with the assistance of her visual aid—a postcard rack, bought an end to our quandary. One side represented a dove, the other side a whale; thus peace returned to La Paz.

We made a boat dive out of La Paz. Los Motes, one of a tiny islet group, at the north end of larger Isla Partida, Sea of Cortez, would be our destination. Los Motes lingered about two-hours off shore. Here, our days of lackluster dive experiences, on this trip, would soon be left behind.

"The elephant seal is in the water," the dive master shouted in excitement. It didn't take long to see why he created such a stir. Sea lions nearly covered the small barren island, except for one elephant seal.

The Sea of Cortez remains one of the cleanest bodies of water in the world, and richest seas. An estimated eight-hundred varieties of fish and three-thousand species (including invertebrates) inhabit the crystal-clear water.

We had the good fortune to have aboard our dive boat a student marine biologist. The future scientist studied the wildlife that made the Sea of Cortez their home. He collected data then turned it over to the Mexican government, to help protect future species.

Sea lions were among the subjects of his studies. He recorded the sounds they intentionally made, and those they did not. "They belch, they fart, just like people," he explained. "The elephant seal is friendly," he continued. "He especially likes bright colors."

We were amazed to see how friendly the elephant seal was. After our dive we were given the chance to jump in and swim with him and the sea lions.

The California sea lions whizzed closely by, their streamlined bodies speeding like bullets past us. If we had our regulators in our mouths, the sea lions might try to tug them out. Generally however, they kept their distance. The elephant seal constituted a different story.

One of the female snorkelers, our friend Trudy, dressed in a hot pink wetsuit, attracted his attention. He barreled toward her full speed ahead. When he reached her, he wrapped his fins around her and gave her a big hug. She scratched under his chin. He tipped his head back a little further. They twirled around and performed a graceful water ballet.

Trudy tired and decided she'd like to sit the next one out. The elephant seal however, was still "in the mood." He grabbed her leg between his fins and didn't appear to have any interest in letting go.

He finally succumbed, and looking a little dejected swam back to shore. With a huge heave-ho he boosted his mammoth body back on shore. He looked up, almost seemed to sigh and then quickly dropped his head to the ground.

Trudy meanwhile had climbed back aboard. We asked her if she was frightened. "Not really," she said. "He was gentle, just like a big teddy bear."

The elephant seal we nick-named Romeo. We found ourselves hoping that one day his Juliet would come along.

Russ, Trudy, Jerry and I made no other dives off Los Motes; the unsurpassable Shakespearean play could have no encore.

Our rented Baja bug lumbered up the peninsula to Mulege; the jalopy's air-conditioning system cranked to high—all four windows were down.

My hair danced about in the breeze, as we sped across the desert—hot, dry and dusty—for hours. An occasional cow or goat wandering across the road interrupted the monotony. Road signs constituted exciting events.

After what seemed like an endless journey, from a hilltop we spied the prize—blue water. Like a magnificent sapphire, a true jewel in the middle of the barren cactus and sage bush desert, the Sea of Cortez reappeared.

Once we returned to the water, we couldn't stay away. Russ and Jerry stopped at almost every opportunity to swim and snorkel. Playa Coyote and El Requeson soon became two of our favorite *playas* (beaches.)

In the course of several shore dives, Jerry and Russ collected a walloping number of clams. Punta Chivato's resort, our northern-most destination had a "YOU CATCH, WE COOK" policy. I figured they probably meant fish, but what the heck, maybe they'd prepare clams too.

Russ and I stopped at the dive shop in Mulege, and told the proprietor about our catch. Her eyes lit up as we described our shiny, brown clams to her. "Those are chocolates. They are very good," she informed us.

Feeling confident, we returned with our heavy goody bags laden with delights. Jerry and Russ presented their finds to the chef. For $5 (US) per person the cook proceeded to prepare a most delicious concoction. He threw in tortilla chips, salsa, salad, fresh vegetable, baked potato, refried beans, and flan. Russ, Jerry, Trudy and I partook of the bounty, until we nearly burst, then raised our Coronas and toasted our *fiesta*, "Here's to the four amigos, and then—*siesta*."

CHAPTER 7

Oughter Dive Monterey and the Channel Islands

The adorable cuddly creature floated on its back in the kelp forest, whacking its tiny paws furiously on its tummy. "What is that little thing *doing*?" I asked Russ.

"That's a sea otter. He's got an abalone on his stomach, and he's using a rock to break it open, so he can eat it."

"Of course, that's exactly what I thought. That has got to be one of the cutest critters I've ever laid eyes on." As if he knew we were talking about him, he stopped pounding, looked up at us and slightly tilted his head to the side.

We sat on the dock at Monterey's Historic Old Fisherman's Wharf that fronted the rocky shore of the Pacific, enchanted by the miniature marine mammal. His home, the Monterey Bay National Marine Sanctuary, covered over 6,000 square miles of ocean. "Wonder what he's going to do next?" I turned to asked Russ.

"Probably enjoy his lunch."

He must have been a wily little guy to catch the mollusk. Awed by how fast they could move; Russ and I had watched red abalone scurry over the rocks. "Warp snail speed," is how Russ described their velocity.

When I glanced back, the furry cutie, an endangered species, had disappeared. He reminded me of something I'd learned in our travels, *carpe diem*. My interpretation: enjoy pleasures as they come along without dwelling on potential consequences. I never wished to regret things I didn't do. At times, sheer luck saved us when we employed this strategy. This happened to be one of those trips.

This part of our beautiful county, in the expansive state of California afforded many wondrous opportunities. Monterey County alone had nearly one-hundred miles of coastline with thirteen exquisite beaches. A shore lover's paradise, all sorts of activities abounded—from beachcombing for super-scarce, red "mermaid's tears" (colorful pieces of beach glass), to watching sea lions rollick on the rocks. Splendid times were limited only by people's imaginations.

Great anticipation swirled around these trips. Diving presented a similar excitement to opening a gift. Until access was gained to the unseen prize, the mystery tantalized. This planned undersea adventure surpassed being tantalizing, it proved terrifying.

The day prior to our arrival, a great white shark assaulted a scuba diver. The sea predator can exceed twenty-feet in length and weight over 5,000 pounds. The diver noticed a large pectoral fin coming toward him, as he sped along on his scuba scooter at about fifty feet. He'd decided to turn around just about the time the shark grabbed him.

After taking a bite, the great white released him. The fortunate diver wore an aluminum console for his work, which protected his abdomen. His steel tank shielded his back. He returned to the boat. Both pieces of hardware had bite marks. He survived, sandwiched in between, however it ended his scuba experience for that day.

We'd heard that such attacks occurred about every five years off the coastal waters of Monterey. I figured if we were lucky, there shouldn't be another incident for four years and 364 days. I recalled a stale scuba joke: If a shark is approaching, you don't have to swim fast; you just have to swim faster than your buddy.

Russ, I, and our friends that had joined us, became somewhat unnerved by the news, but decided to go ahead with our plans. We found ourselves alone on Monastery Beach, the same one where the shark ambush occurred the day before.

Monastery Beach in Carmel River State Beach lay between Monterey and Carmel in a scenic section of coastline. A favorite boarding location when surf raged. If calm, it made for great diving. It existed in close proximity to Point Lobos. The marine reserve provided a safe refuge and healthy home for a diverse population of indigenous inhabitants.

Fellow divers called the site, Mortuary Beach. Russ thought the nickname was applied due to the extreme steep slope of the beach and high surf. I began to wonder. Exiting the water proved difficult if the surf was up. Divers frequently had to bow to nature and crawl out on their hands and knees. The possibility of being slapped back into the abyss represented a real threat.

The puny courageous, or stupid, group of us entered the water. The sandy shore gave way to rocks as we descended. Color and fish life surrounded us. Bull kelp thrived. Young red abalone crawled on boulders. When we disturbed them, they scooted. In addition to the mollusks, we also glimpsed several types of anemones, rockfish, sea perch, and sea urchins—another favorite sea otter snack.

The shallow dive, forty-foot maximum depth, teemed with sea life. Fifty-foot visibility allowed us to partake of the marine gallery. The kelp forest provided a lush undersea environment for a variety of species. After enjoying a spectacular dive; we humbled ourselves to the cosmos and exited the water.

"Outrageous dive. I'm so glad we decided to go for it," I gushed. *Carpe diem*, I thought. We'd "seized the day" and hadn't let fear dissuade us from making one glorious cold water dive.

When I now recall the joy of the experience; I remain happy we made the dive, and even happier to be sitting here writing this.

Our group made two other shore dives in the area, the Coast Guard

Pier and the oceanfront of Green Gables Inn.

The Coast Guard Pier, a classic beginning's dive failed to enthrall us. The good thing though, as with many novice sites, ease typified it. Everyone suited up at their leisure, in the parking lot adjacent to the dock entry. A small store and restrooms came in handy for a couple of quick stops.

Stellar sea lions frequented the north side of the pier. The weight of the massive sea mammals sunk docks and damaged boats. The protected status the animals enjoyed prevented impacted people from taking action. So, the big fellows—who might have been considered by some obtrusive, noisy and bad smelling—lounged at their leisure barking belly laughs at their detractors.

In an easy entry, we walked backwards down the beach, into calm water. At forty-feet underwater scenery and fish life were minimal. The harbor seals whizzing by created the most memorable aspect of the dive. As Russ pointed out, keeping in mind the presence of the great white shark, "Seeing large light-colored objects coming toward us—scary."

Green Gables Inn, a Queen Ann Victorian bed-and-breakfast, situated along side the coastal highway, served as the jumping off point for our next dive. We parked by the road, then stumbled down a hill and over rocks to reach the shore.

Russ, our diving friends and I, made a shallow descent into a kelp forest, fighting the surge the entire way. A rip current and one-to-two-foot swells dogged us throughout the dive. The restless sea only allowed perhaps twenty-five feet of visibility.

"Well, nothing like jumping into a washing machine every now and then." I felt like a piece of wet laundry as we climbed the bank to the highway.

"Come on, we'll get out of these damp clothes then you can feel complete, like you just got out of the dryer," Russ said.

Although the sea lions may have been stellar, the shore diving in the immediate vicinity wasn't. We tried a boat dive. A short ride, about one mile north of Point Lobos landed us at the Pinnacle site. Divers made a steep descent into ninety feet of gloomy water. A pinnacle, covered with orange encrusting sponges, illuminated the darkness like an undersea lighthouse beacon. Even with the huge flashlight, we didn't see much.

As Russ and I later discovered on a number of our trips, the diving at times, became secondary to the destination. We loved Monterey. Four of our friends and fellow divers, accompanied us on this jaunt. A stunning natural setting beside the Pacific Ocean, and an invigorating sea breeze, set the stage for a good time.

Many activities, besides the diving, existed. The Monterey Aquarium, an outstanding facility, beckoned. "Why? We just saw everything out in the ocean," Russ protested.

"Because," I reasoned, "We wouldn't have to worry about the great white." Besides, I enjoyed seeing the undersea ecosystem without being shivering cold.

The setting of the aquarium, located on Cannery Row, seemed appropriate. John Steinbeck received the inspiration for his novel about the sardine industry there. Today the canneries have been replaced by tourist attractions; restaurants, shops and hotels.

From Cannery Row we pondered whether to stroll, or rent four-wheel surrey bikes and peddle the scenic trail to Fisherman's Wharf. We opted to amble along the route that fronted the bay. Walking the path enabled us to stop and admire the considerable sea life and wild life that populated the shore.

Our happy group wrapped up our visit to Monterey with a meal at a Chinese restaurant. As our party was being seated at a large round table, I noticed a *Maneki Neko*—good luck cat—slowly waving a raised paw at us.

"Guess, he must have been with us all the time," I said. A few people laughed.

The fortune cookies arrived. Russ read his, and then looked around the room.

"What did it say?" one of our friends asked.

"'You will live a long life.' I didn't figure it was meant for our table." Everyone laughed that time.

Russ and I headed down Highway 101 S; everyone else returned home.

We arrived in Santa Barbara, about 200 miles to the south, the night prior to our scheduled dive.

Truth Aquatics ran three boats, each longer than sixty-five-feet; *Truth, Vision* and *Conception.* After locating our boat, we loaded our gear onto it. The live-aboard ship had been outfitted for the comfort of divers. Russ and I found a cozy bunk, threw our sleeping bags on it, and got snug for the evening.

Sometime during the night, the captain swung the large craft away from the dock, and pointed the bow toward the Channel Islands. We awoke to a sunny day with a moderate breeze, and a huge appetite. Our group of twenty-divers, or at least the ones who got up, met for breakfast at the topside galley.

Shortly after the morning meal, *Conception* arrived at Santa Cruz of the Channel Islands—the only one of the eight isles we dove. The rocky shoreline that encircled the wild, uninhabited island created its most noticeable feature. Oil derricks in a straight line marched down the channel.

The skipper bought the watercraft to a halt, anchoring in a waveless sea.

Our group made two dives at a site dubbed Pelican Point. Looking around, we guessed it was for the birds, the name that is.

The first dive, at a former abalone collecting haven, when it remained legal, had patches of bull kelp and diverse marine fauna. Visibility ranged from forty feet to sixty feet. Bright light infiltrated the sun-blocking bull kelp and created sparkling highlights in contrast to it. A few lonely abalones skittered around on rocks near shore.

Our second dive, another shallow descent, a short distance from the first on the shoreline, resembled the initial descent. Giant keyhole limpets proved the outstanding feature of this exploration. A globby-looking, grayish mantle covered the oval shell. They looked like a melted doorknob with the lock slightly off center.

After a pleasant descent, each of us climbed back aboard and enjoyed a hot shower, followed by the juice and cookies.

On the return trip the wind had freshened. The channel became a sea of whitecaps. As we departed the captain bellowed, his voice carried on the gale, "Hold on. If the chairs fall over, don't bother to pick them up." As he leaned into the wind, moving across the deck, holding his hat, it quickly became clear any such effort would only result in futility. Divers and crew braced ourselves for a much slower return trip.

The big boat seemed much smaller on the way back to Santa Barbara. Monumental size waves drove over the bow. White water soared into the air. Russ and I, anticipating the potential rough seas, had taken Dramamine prior to departure. We didn't get seasick, but almost everyone else did. I felt fine, however when I looked around at the green gills and I-think-I've-got-to-lean-over-the-rail mugs, I couldn't help but feel sorry for them.

My buddy and I went to the front of the vessel and rode the bow like the couple in the shipwreck movie. We rose toward the sky, and then dashed into the furrows between the waves. The swells subsided, as the skipper approached the harbor late afternoon.

"Well, Suzy we made it back. What did you think of that?" Russ asked.

"I think it reflected life and diving—lots of ups and downs, but more highs than lows.

What's up next? I wondered. I couldn't wait to find out.

CHAPTER 8

Fiji—The True Beauty

"We'll be making a quick stop. Have a special delivery," announced the swarthy pilot of the twin-otter aircraft. The Fijian archipelago has over 300 islands, about one-third inhabited; all have celebrations. If required, Sunflower Airlines took the cake. After our unscheduled jaunt, total flight time exceeded twenty-seven hours. Over 14,000 frequent flyer miles had been logged before touching down at Taveuni.

The Garden Isle provided us with many pleasant memories. Two sisters, Sainiana Adimaiwai, the eldest and Kesaia Emi, the younger—created one of those for me.

One afternoon I set out on foot, to find the Waitavala Natural Water Slide—a local attraction just down the road from the resort. As I wandered along the dirt road, clouds began forming overhead. In a tropical rainforest, and lacking any gecko luck, I soon found myself drenched. The dust beneath my feet turned to muck.

"*Bula*!" (Hello) Two young girls returning from school greeted me in their native language. Fiji's seasons are opposite of ours; it was their last day of classes for the year.

"*Ausalakokivei*?" (Where are you going) They wanted to know. Islanders seemed interested in my destination. This might be, because when you live on a small island, there are only so many places you can go.

"I thought I'd try to find the water slide."

"We will take you there," the older sister said. A huge smile accompanied her offer.

That we were going in opposite directions, that liquid sunshine enveloped us, or that they were beginning their vacations, didn't seem to matter.

"I would like that." How nice of them, I thought.

The "just down the road" attraction turned out to be a strenuous hike up a slippery mountainside. The three of us followed the trail through dense brush, amidst dangling vines. The serpentine path ascended, and then disappeared into the jungle.

The girls and I chatted, when I could catch my breath, as we trudged along on our arduous trek. The siblings were curious about things off their wee home. Did I have a husband, kids and pets? What was life like in "the States?" How long would I be there? Where was I going after I left? They listened with great interest. Their eyes seemed to swell to the size of loofah sponges as they attempted to absorb it all.

After I'd satisfied their enormous curiosities, they begin sharing their lives with me.

As the sisters scampered up the slope, they'd dutifully glance back. If I lagged too far behind, my young guides would pause and wait for me to catch up.

The siblings delivered me to the water slide, and then presented me with a most impressive performance. After climbing up the rocks, they doffed their *sulu's*, then leapt into one of connecting pools that cascaded down the steep peak.

I stood in awe of the beautiful, careful souls that frolicked in the water before me. I pondered what Sainiana, the older sister had told me. "We have no crime here. We can come and go without worry." I wondered in how many places on earth someone could feel that safe.

I told them I had to go, although, I actually never wanted to leave. They scrambled back up on the rocks. Fetching their sulus, they tied them on. Faces aglow, dripping with water and adorned with those wonderful Fijian smiles, they accompanied me back through the jungle. They insisted on walking me back to the resort.

"We need to get your address, so we can write letters," Sainiana said.

Whether we correspond or not is unimportant, for on that day, they touched me more than words ever could have.

I returned to the resort, anxious to tell Russ about my new friends, and hungry enough to eat him. "Let's go to the Cannibal Café," I suggested.

"Sounds good, um, well, that sounds okay."

We walked around the building. On the beach, four mismatched plastic tables with white and green chairs, scattered in disarray, created a casual dining area. They sat underneath an oversized, thatched, palm frond roof. One diner sat eating fish and rice. To the back, a huge banner, oddly obscuring the view, announced: CANNIBAL CAFÉ "We'd love to have you for dinner."

"Would you mind taking a picture of us later?" I asked the other guest as we passed by.

"No problem," he said, and then returned to his meal.

"Wonder how many tourists they've had for dinner?" Russ asked.

"Well, I dunno, but looks like there's only one left."

Russ dragged a table across the sand, to create a view of the water; then pulled up a couple of chairs.

I grabbed a worn, paper menu from a napkin holder. Excessive use made it difficult to read. "Looks like it's going to be fish and rice," I said after perusing the available selection. "I'm not getting the pork. Sitting here under this covering, with a name like this place has, makes me feel like I'm an *imu* pit. I don't want to be what's for dinner."

"Ready for your picture?" the apparent survivor inquired, as he approached our table.

"Sure," I said, handing him the camera. We stood in front of the sign, biting our arms.

The camera clicked off the shot. "Thanks," I said. He handed the SLR back and left.

"They didn't have him for dinner."

"May have been something wrong with his taste buds, maybe he didn't taste good," Russ said. A droll smile crept across his face as we headed back to our room.

"The place where the new day begins" is Fiji's tagline. The International Date Line has been relocated so all Fijian islands lie to the west of it. The next morning we strolled to the tiny village of Wairiki. A stately, worn stucco building with a grand facade caught our eye. Emblazoned upon it in fresh dark paint—180th Meridian.

I grabbed a palm frond and dragged it across the gravel road to create a boundary. "Oh, look." I hopped over the divider. "It's yesterday. We can eat Thanksgiving dinner again." Then I remembered how stuffed I was. "No, better not do that." I hopped back. "It's pretty cool getting to choose what day you want it to be."

As Russ and I ambled toward the beach; local fisherman headed out to sea. Whatever the catch, it would probably be dinner.

On our way to the village of Somosomo, we passed over a one-lane bridge that spanned a rushing stream. The sleepy isle, that occasionally yawned when a rooster crowed, abruptly awoke. The din of dozens of kids whooping it up in the creek, trumped all other sounds. "*Ausalakokivei?*" an *au naturel* three-year old asked, pausing just long enough to hear the answer.

"Somosomo," I said, surprising myself that I knew the answer.

He looked content with my reply. He climbed back up the rocks to execute another flying leap into the water. The clamor of the rollicking youngsters faded as we neared town.

Russ rented a 4WD Jeep, one of the two rental vehicles on the island at the time.

Des Voeux Peak, Taveuni's second highest mountain would be our destination. Two sinewy, sweaty, barefoot natives toting king-size burlap bags trudged along the road. The burdens sat atop their shoulders, pushing their heads askew. "Wonder what's in those?"

"*Kava*—the dried root of a pepper plant, maybe?" Russ guessed.

As we climbed the mountain, it began to sprinkle. Farther up, into the rain forest, misty precipitation intensified into a drenching downpour. Raindrops the size of sand dollars hit the windshield. Vegetation changed. Tree ferns the size of redwoods began appearing. Coconut palms filled the remaining available canopy.

The damp lushness of the scenery through our fogged, rain-splattered Jeep window, made it seem as though we were being swallowed by a giant, misty cloud.

"Grab the camcorder. Let's get some video." Russ was anxious to play with his new toy.

"OK." *I don't know about this*, I thought.

The higher we went, the worst the road got. The roadbed, slathered in potholes and erosion ditches, would have been impassable, if not for the four-wheel drive.

"Whoa." As I attempted to start filming, Russ hit a depression large enough to swallow a vehicle. I bounced up nearly high enough to rebound off the roof. The camera jiggled up and down. Suddenly it occurred to me how inane this idea was. I started laughing. I'd almost stop, and then we'd hit another hole. I couldn't stop laughing as the jeep jostled me.

"What's so funny?'

"Oh, nothing."

We reached an altitude where the rambling goat trail turned into a mountain stream.

"Well, I guess we're going to have to turn around here," Russ said.

"That's okay," I said, in between chortles. "I think I have enough footage." I meant pictures of my feet.

That evening a *Yaqona* (*kava*) ceremony followed dinner. Guests gathered in the open-air lobby of the hotel. The chairs, arranged in a circle surrounded a stump. On it sat a shallow, *tanoa* (hand-carved wooden bowl). Bare-chested men attired in *sulus* (sarongs), sat cross-legged near the bowl. Women sat behind them.

"Have a grog with us," the handsome Fijian invited attendees, as he unwrapped a piece of cloth over the vessel. White powder spilled out. He mixed it in water. He poured the muddy-looking liquid into a *bilo* (coconut shell half) and passed it to first person.

With one clap, the *bilo* was accepted with a *bula* by the guest, who clapped three times in appreciation. The *bilo* continued to be passed around until the *tanoa* was emptied.

It wasn't necessary to drink every *bilo* offered, but courtesy mandated partaking in at least the first round.

"Yeech," I whispered to Russ. "That has got to be about the worst tasting stuff ever." I declined further offers. Russ continued to accept the *bilo* and went through several rounds of *bulas*.

"You know, after you drink enough of this, it's not so bad, but my lips are going numb," Russ muttered to me.

"I think maybe you should pass next time. We don't know what the heck that stuff is. Don't know what else might go numb."

Russ clapped three final times, and made that his last round.

The evening continued well into the night. A number of island residents arrived, including our buddies from the dive shop. Several men grabbed guitars and sang in their native language, mellow and melodic. *Kava* and music wound the fete down gently, like a finely tuned timepiece.

As the moonlight lit up the starry sky, we stumbled back to the room, Russ still fingering his lips. *Kava*, we later discovered is a mild narcotic.

Russ and I slept in the next morning and arrived late to our pre-arranged dive.

Scuba shop employees, tanks thrown over their shoulders, were already wading out to greet the approaching boat. The red dive flag flapped in the breeze, creating a striking contrast to the cloudless blue sky. The dive master and skipper bantered in Fijian and laughed. Their camaraderie seemed more indicative of play than work.

Divers followed the good-natured crew to the boat. Their jollity affected us like a rampant infection. A party-like sense of merriment befell. Fellowship set the day's tone.

"Did you guys see that shark?" I said, as I pulled my mask off. "He must have been that, no that long," As my hands were freed, I stretched my arms out to indicate how big, and then spread them wider. "At least, twelve feet long."

"Yeah, a grey reef shark" a diver across from me chimed in. He sported a backwards ball cap, reclined with his arms spread over the rail, and his legs stretched out in front of him. "No, actually he might have been fourteen or fifteen feet long."

"And, you have to remember, everything looks smaller underwater." Enough laughter reverberated through the boat to nearly capsize it. When the guffaws abated, I added, "The rest of you guys didn't see him, because I shooed him off."

"Seriously, that dive was utterly spectacular. I've never seen so much color on a dive ever," my fellow man-eater estimator, said. "Soft corals, hard corals, sponges, fish, turtle, anemones, giant clams, crinoids. Too much to see."

"We found the pot of gold and the rainbow—deep-purple violet to fire-engine red, and every hue in between," I said.

"Have to admit," Russ injected, "It was A1."

Perhaps we shouldn't have been so awed by the first-rate diving. I'd read Fiji's reefs provided home to hundreds of coral species, both hard and soft; sponges and sea fans. Fish and other marine inhabitants, such as the mollusks and crustaceans added further variety.

Hope, I never decide to write about this, I mused. I would have no idea, how to describe such indescribable beauty.

Fiji won our, "Favorite-Place-to-Dive-Award: South Pacific" designation. Having experienced, what we considered, some of the finest diving on the planet, we found to be both good and bad. Diving Tavenui spoiled us forever. "You can't beat that. Let's go explore another island," I suggested.

The accommodating hotel staff prepared us a couple of box lunches, and loaned us a cooler. Arrangements were made for a day trip to Korolevu Island, aka Haunted Island.

The boat skipped over the water like a stone. As we neared the shore, the captain slowed to a stop, then killed the engine. My buddy and I leapt off the back of the craft, masks and fins in hand, into waist-high, bath water. The clear water made it possible to see the white sand bottom and small fry swimming around us.

We water-walked, lifting our knees high against the pressure of the surf to the beach.

The deserted isle belonged to us to 4 P.M. Russ and I moseyed around the island, stopping along the way to snorkel. When the sun was directly overhead, I found a palm tree that provided shade. We got comfortable on a driftwood log, underneath the palm. I unboxed our lunches and we munched our sandwiches, staring out to sea.

My focus returned to the beach when I placed a wad of crumpled plastic wrap back in the cooler. "A coconut. That would make a good desert. I like coconut."

"Okay, then, you open it."

"You know, I can never get those things open. Will you help me?" I whined, but stopped short of begging.

"No."

"Oh, come on. I know you can."

"Okay, I'll try."

The whir of a motor, four hours later announced the return of the boat. The coconut sat unopened. I grabbed the coconut and flung it as far out to sea as I could. "I don't like coconuts anymore. That takes care of that." I wiped my hands together.

A feeling of satisfaction swept over me. The irritating, brown menace would haunt me no more. "Maybe, that's why they call this the Haunted Island—coconuts! That one should be on its way to China."

"Wrong sea." Russ was always so darn accurate.

"Well, somewhere other than here. That's good enough for me."

I went to retrieve our snorkel gear. As I turned around, out of the corner of my eye I caught a glimpse of—the coconut. The incoming tide had returned the woody bedevilment.

I slogged out, retrieved it, and did my best javelin toss to again send it on its way again.

I waited.

The boat arrived and the skipper motioned for us to return. As we handed our gear up, I watched. Russ and I climbed aboard. The captain started the motor and began to pull away. I felt a smile spread across my face. I looked back at the rooster's tail shooting into the air. My eyes followed it down to the water. There it was, floating not three feet from the vessel—the coconut.

"You know what I'd like to do today," I said the next morning. "I think I'd like to go somewhere there were no coconuts."

"On Tavenui, I don't think that's possible."

"Okay then, let's go face the demon head-on. Let's go hiking in the coconut palms. Tavaro Falls has lots of them, and big tree ferns too."

And so it was, we were on our way to the falls. Sweltering, muggy rainforest enveloped us as we lumbered up the steep hill. A knotted rope stretched across a zigzag stream. My buddy and I took turns hanging on it, as we selectively balanced ourselves on sizeable boulders to cross the creek. The rope, somewhat lax, swung back and forth.

"Be careful Suzy," Russ admonished, just as I lost my balance and fell on my bottom.

Overheated and exhausted at the end of the trail, we arrived at a one-hundred-foot, thundering waterfall. "I'm hot. I'm going for a swim." I jumped in the pool and began swimming toward the pounding stream of water.

"Suzy…"

The turbulent energy shocked me. It swirled all around me. It pulled me down. I surfaced only long enough to get a gasp of air, before being drawn down again. I reversed direction and swam as fast as I could, to escape the powerful force. I made it back to shore and dragged myself out.

"Suzy, are you all right?" Russ sounded concerned. Seeing I was okay, he said, "That was a pretty dumb thing to do."

"I guess so. But, I'm not too hot now, and there weren't any coconuts out there."

Jerry's Jelly dive site, anemone and clownfish enjoy a symbiotic relationship. Taveuni, Fiji

CHAPTER 9

Cook Islands—Don't Hold Your Breath Tangaroa

Impatient passengers milled about. Some thumbed through magazines, while others opted to sit and watch people go by. Children, who had been cooped up too long, like chickens in a pen, chased one another around the black leather seats.

"How much longer do you think it might be?" a fellow passenger asked the reservation clerk.

"We have no way of knowing sir. We'll be underway as soon as possible."

We gazed out the gate window at Portland International Airport, watching snow fall on the mechanics. They'd been attempting to repair a frozen wing de-icer valve for an hour and a-half. Ironically, the amount of time we had to make our connecting flight from Los Angeles to the Cook Islands.

The repair completed, we taxied onto the runway and received clearance for take off. Our arrival in LA, two-hours late, sent us sprinting in vain toward the International Terminal. Two elated stand-by passengers now occupied our seats on the closed-door aircraft.

"I can't believe it," I groaned. We stood and looked in disbelief at the 747 through the glass terminal wall, feeling like little kids that had their toys stolen by the Grinch.

After dealing with the disappointment, we faced the reality of the situation. Russ spent a considerable amount of time on the phone. Extensive negotiation enabled us to reschedule our flight and accommodations.

Because of the islands' remote location, only a few departures weekly were scheduled for the Cooks. We either had to lose or add several days of vacation.

"I think I'd prefer to add a couple of days," Russ said.

"Me too. Let's go to San Diego." To make the best of the remaining two days until the next flight, my buddy and I headed south. A certain amount of psychic discord swirled about, as we stood looking at tropical vegetation at the San Diego Zoo. I'd anticipated seeing it, but not there.

Eventually my partner and I found ourselves back in LA and on the plane.

"Ladies and gentlemen: please stow all electronic devices, ensure your seat backs are in an upright position and your tray tables are locked away," the flight attendant went through her usual spiel over the P.A. system. We sipped our drinks and munched our peanuts as we thumbed through the in-flight magazines.

The pilot welcomed us aboard. "Good morning, ladies and gentlemen. The skies are calm and the conditions look good for a quick flight into Tahiti today."

Tahiti!? I dropped the magazine and my mouth followed. This time we'd actually made it on a jumbo jet, but our final destination—wrong.

"Excuse me, miss. I believe we're on the wrong flight," I said grabbing the attention of attendant as she hurried down the aisle with her props for the seat belt and life vest demonstration.

"That can't be possible. Your destination is Tahiti. Is that not correct?"

"Yes, that is not correct. We're trying to get to the Cook Islands. We're not having good luck."

She quickly shuffled us off the plane. We returned to the reservation clerk. "It does appear that there has been a small error."

Small error? More like a several thousand mile miss. The airline offered their profuse apologies. They then got us on the next flight, with a first class upgrade, to the Cooks.

"Those are the kind of mistakes I like," I said reclining in my plush seat. I dabbed at my face with the warm cloth scented with fresh lemon, while sipping complimentary white wine from a crystal stemmed goblet. I planned to read my USA Today after I'd finished my chef prepared entrée.

"Chicken or ponds?" the primly dressed Air New Zealand attendant inquired, interrupting my planning. Outfitted in a cornflower blue, double-breasted suit, accessorized with an ascot and bowler, she presented a polished appearance.

"*Chicken or ponds?*" I thought to myself. Feeling hungrier than thirsty, I decided to go with the chicken.

"Seafood," she said, as if reading my mind. Perhaps my quizzical look gave me away. "Ponds are seafood."

I pondered for awhile, and then a light bulb came on. "Oh, I get it. Prawns."

We'd had our first exposure to the sort of pronunciation we'd be hearing often on this trip.

"You know, this is the life. I always wondered what went on 'the other side of the curtain,'" I said. "So this is how the other half lives."

"Don't get too use to it. We aren't always lucky enough to be so unlucky."

First class proved comfortable enough. We fell asleep and slept through most of the eighteen-hour flight. "Fresh towelette?" the attentive stewardess offered, arousing us from our slumber.

"Don't mind if I do," I replied, as I noticed dawn breaking outside the window.

The smell of freshly brewed coffee filled the cabin and began bringing people back to life. Before we knew it, the landing gear dropped and the wheels hit the tarmac.

Ah, we finally made it. The Cook Islands appeared to be a paradise beyond description. Our perception may have been influenced by our difficulties, but still the tropical splendor inspired euphoria.

The islanders, friendly and gracious, created part of the enchantment. Infectious smiles and a gentle manner endeared us to them in no time at all. Quick wits and great senses of humor made for enjoyable chats.

"We didn't know what the truck was saying," lamented one of the two sisters who owned the beach front cottage where we stayed. She had just returned from "the States" and bought back a toy, a talking semi-truck for her sons.

A serendipitous event occurred. A truck driver from California happened to be vacationing there. The sisters were delighted to find out what the truck said, "That's a big ten-four good buddy."

They laughed as they rejoiced in their newly found knowledge. Then one of them turned to me and asked, "But what does that mean?"

I attempted to explain, but realized I didn't know either. We all laughed more.

Islanders speak English, Maori—the native language, and French Polynesian. They're delightful to listen to. Although they look Polynesian, they sound like New Zealanders.

Other ties to New Zealand became evident upon our departure from the airport. Driving is on the left side—or a helpful local might remind Russ, "Hey mate, you're riding down the wrong side of the road!"

"How many times did you turn the windshield wipers on?" a

fellow vacationer asked. More times than we cared to admit, since all the controls were reversed, it happened often.

Russ didn't need to turn on the wipers at all; on Raratonga and Aitutaki it rained only once for fifteen minutes. The entire rest of the time we basked in a sunny eighty to eighty-five degrees.

Currency, the New Zealand dollar, is good news for American tourists. The exchange rate hovered around .5556. That meant that we doubled our money when we exchanged our traveler's checks.

The bad news, however, is that basically everything has to be imported—primarily from New Zealand—so everything is expensive.

Russ and I decided to try and save money by cooking in our cottage. I had to search through several scant home-front stores until I found a package of frozen chicken franks. The hot dogs cost eight dollars (*$NZ*) and the mustard four dollars (*$NZ*). After that we started eating a lot of bread and fruit.

I'd slather butter on bread and team it with tropical produce for breakfast. Fruit varied: papayas, bananas, pineapples and oranges—which were actually green. Sweet delicious flavor burst forth from all. The econo-meal gave us a good start.

"Funny, haven't seen anyone eat a coconut," I said. Coconut palms grew almost everywhere, but residents didn't seem to consider them a food source.

"We mostly feed them to the pigs," an islander told us.

Agriculture in the islands consisted of meager family owned farms—we'd call them gardens. Taro, a main staple, had edible roots, as well as spinach-like leaves. Bananas shined as another favorite, along with a juicy little watermelon, about the size of a cantaloupe.

Farm animals wandered the islands—cows, goats, pigs, and chickens. If we might be contemplating dinner, we received a friendly warning from a resident, "Be careful mates—everybody knows who owns 'em!"

The need for islanders to grow their own food became apparent. "If they say we are out of sugar, they will get more—but the price might temporarily double or triple because it has to be air-freighted in," a local woman informed us.

The other alternative would be to wait three or more months, until a rusty freighter made its way from New Zealand. We noticed during our time there—the smaller the island, the higher the price.

My buddy and I made one dive on Raratonga—a wild one. A storm front had just passed through. The surf pounded, as our group of eight—nine including Dave the dive master—loaded a twenty-foot hard-bottomed inflatable raft with tanks, weight belts and the rest of our gear.

"Hurry up mates. We don't want the conditions to get any worse," Dave shouted over the roar of the ocean.

The islands—coral atolls, are surrounded by an outside fringing reef. Inside the reef the water is shallow and calm, great for snorkeling, but lousy for diving.

Diving necessitated getting outside of the fringing reef.

The waves crashed down and created a dangerous undertow. Dave evaluated the situation, "The conditions aren't looking any better." He had ambivalent feelings about making the crossing at all, but decided, "You only live once mates. Let's give it a go."

I wondered if the term "lunatic fringe" originated to describe someone making such decisions. A no guts, no glory attitude seemed to prevail.

Getting through the passage required a considerable amount of expertise and a bit of foolhardiness. "Hold on mates," Dave bellowed as the raft pitched and rolled with ten-to-twenty-foot waves breaking underneath us. Swells of seven-to-ten feet tossed the inflatable about like a rag doll in a lion's mouth.

Cold spray flew back and slapped me in the face. I could taste the salt on my lips and feel the sting in my eyes. Divers held on for dear life as the nose of the raft crested, then dropped down, time and time again, in the violent ocean.

Then, just as sudden as it begun, it ended. The group had survived the Papua Passage. Dave summarized the experience, "There was no room for error."

The dive master attempted to anchor, but the surrounding rough water made it impossible. He proceeded farther out, away from the reef, where he could secure the raft.

Exquisite one-hundred-foot visibility greeted us. The crystal-clear blue water sparkled in the sun. Surge, from the unsettled water, took us on an exhilarating joyride. Divers were carried along an extensive reef, which teemed with life.

Our next challenge?—to avoid being thrown into a coral head.

Since the water temperature exceeded eighty degrees, our protective clothing proved less than adequate. An encounter with a coral head could be nasty. Safety necessitated caution to avoid cuts and scrapes that could become infected.

Our bottom time flew by as fast as the surge that carried us. Before we knew it, we had spent our allowed thirty minutes at eighty feet.

Time arrived to ascend. Near the surface we paused at twenty feet, for a decompression stop. Divers more than sixty feet below us were clearly visible. Their bubbles floated up, creating billowing, translucent hydra-like creatures.

Dave maneuvered the boat back toward shore. Divers remained optimistic, with fingers crossed. In a stroke of good luck, the sea had calmed down. The passage back gently returned us to shore, a welcome contrast from our trip out.

Russ and I enjoyed a late afternoon stroll down a deserted white sand beach, savoring the sensation of our après dive. Barefooted, flip-flops in hand, I stopped for a moment to appreciate the beauty. Couldn't dawdle too long though—Raratonga was about to be rocked by Island Night. Returning to our cottage, we readied ourselves for the fete.

Exotic, beautiful women with long, blue-black hair swung their hips as bare-chested, Adonis-like men, glistening with sweat, beat on ancestral drums. The women, dressed in coconut shell bras, long grass shirts, and ornamental head gear, waved bright parrot feather fans while casting come hither looks and shy glances. The excitement reached a fevered pitch. With one final bang on the drum, the women dropped to the ground.

"Now, that's what I call entertainment," Russ commented. His huge admiration for the coconut women became readily apparent.

"Yep, those guys beat a mean drum."

Island Night ignited an island-wide celebration. It began with drinks, usually Cook's Lager—a local favored brew, or a sweet tropical umbrella drink such as a Mai Tai. The libations were followed by a buffet featuring: local foods, Polynesian dancers and island music. A festive mood prevailed; the ambience constituted pure delight.

The buffet included a variety of choices. Different and unusual items overspread the long table. I selected food that looked familiar, and tended to avoid unrecognizable items. Baby octopus, goat, and pa-pa pudding were among the identifiable delicacies.

The evening wound down, as did we. Russ and I stumbled off to bed.

The next morning, the whir of an adjustable prop plane, droned in our ears. Air Raratonga's island hopper transported us to Aitutaki, a small island 160 miles to the north.

The pilot and co-pilot studied a karate manual as they flew along, interrupting their studies only long enough to re-trim the plane when necessary for altitude changes. After we'd been there for awhile, we understood why no air scans were necessary. They were the only air traffic; the sound of the flight coming and going, generated excitement island-wide.

The small aircraft touched down on an airstrip that came into use during World War II. It was built across the top of the tiny island, because it would fit there.

After checking into our accommodations, Russ rented a scooter to explore.

"Look out for the chicken!" I yelled. Russ veered the rented scooter around the hen, a near miss.

A fragrant, warm breeze embraced us, as we sped around on our mighty machine. "How you doing Motor Mouse?" Russ reached back to rub my leg.

"Just fine, thank you." I enjoyed every moment.

Scooters were an integral part of Aitutakian's daily life. What they could transport on them astounded us—everything from groceries to scuba tanks.

My initial impression: Aitutaki differed from Raratonga. If Raratonga reminded me of Kona, Hawaii, then Aitutaki reminded me of Baja, Mexico.

The quiet destination had a handful of cozy family-owned resorts equipped with ten rooms or less. Miniature markets, owned by islanders to supplement their incomes, existed in their homes. Locals also grew their own food.

My buddy and I located a dive shop, one that didn't make us carry our tanks on a scooter. We made arrangements to go out the next day.

A dilapidated, hand-made, wooden clunker of a truck, with faded, peeling orange paint showed up the next morning. It consisted of a front seat and flat bed.

"Morning mateys and how are you both, this fine day?" Neil, the friendly former New Zealander inquired. He jumped off the truck to help us load our gear. His fair skin, ripe as a watermelon, and baby-blues gave away his nationality.

"Well, and excited about going diving. Thank you," I replied. After getting everything loaded, Russ and I joined Neil in the front of his open-air wonder.

The hop to the boat launch took ten-minutes.

Neil launched into calm seas. The trip out seemed effortless, compared to Raratonga's harrowing passage.

In a short time, we arrived at Fish Spot, the dive site. Neil anchored. My partner and I donned our gear, suited up, and with a giant step, hit the water.

Fish, of various size and description, surrounded us. A pint-size white-tip shark that glided by grabbed my attention.

As often happens, when I focus on something of interest, I tend to loose track of my bearings. Before I knew it, a gauge check informed me, I'd reached one-hundred-and-two-feet. Oops, that edged toward making me uncomfortable—although it still fell within what is generally acknowledged as the safe limit.

I felt a tug on my wet suit. Russ to the rescue, he always had my back. On multiple occasions I've been thankful I've had him around.

"Those are fish!" I never saw anything like it. On the way back to shore, we witnessed an amazing sight, flying fish. They jumped out of the water, at least a foot high, and then using their fins like wings, sailed through the air.

Maybe the puddle hopping pilots should have paid more attention. There might have been more air traffic than they thought.

Pulling the boat ashore at the wharf; Neil, Russ and I ran into a fishermen who had landed a two-hundred-and-fifty-pound dog-tooth tuna. It covered the entire bottom of his boat.

"Fish on!" he radioed in to the resort, as soon as he landed it. It sold immediately. "Quite a blast, landing that one, you know," the angler proclaimed, bursting with pride at his jewel.

Life is a blast, I thought. What more could one ask of life—than to experience and enjoy it? I found once again, that constituted the real treasure.

Sue, on the dive boat,
peeling off her wetsuit after enjoying a great dive.
Aitutaki, Cook Islands, South Pacific

Post- Kava celebration. Sue and islander kicking up their heels.
Aitutaki, Cook Islands

CHAPTER 10

From Atiu, With Love

A crystal-clear, brilliant blue wave came crashing down with a booming thud. Whitewater spilled over the coral, ebbed, and then headed back out to sea. The pristine paradise, hugged by the close-in fringing reef, paradoxically generated a feeling of tranquility.

"Awesome, peaceful place," I commented, as Russ and I sat watching nature's wondrous show. My wonder however, had a bittersweet bite. As mesmerizing as the violent surf might be to watch, it would make diving impossible.

Disappointment threatened. I'd been looking forward to cave diving, a somewhat rare opportunity. We'd have to be creative, as we had on other trips when the weather failed to co-operate, and figure out other things to do.

"Let's go for walk and look around," I suggested. Hopping up and dusting the sand off my bottom, I set out.

Broken coral rubble and shell fragments littered the deserted beach. Sand trails left by wayward mollusks hinted at life on the lonely shore. Past the beach, craggy, low, black cliffs defined the landscape. A mysterious jungle lay beyond those. The intriguing landscape seduced me. "Come on Russ." I rushed ahead.

I soon found myself in a semi-dense jungle. Miniature crabs went scurrying as I stepped onto a sandy, overgrown path. The fiddle-footed critters scampered off sideways, each disappearing into one of the many holes awaiting their return.

"Russell, you've got to see this. Scads of tiny crabs are everywhere."

As I roamed farther, the sound of the crashing waves grew distant. A harmonious blend of birds, like a welcoming symphony, gained my attention.

"Are you coming?" I tried summoning Russ again.

The jungle, now dense, strangled by hanging vines and highlighted by tropical flora, had a magical feeling about it. It was almost as if the trees were about to become uprooted, and start dancing around like the mushrooms in Fantasia.

The trees had distinctive features. One eye-catching species looked like expert contortionists. They bent, twisted, and swirled in differing directions. Elevated, broad roots protruding out of the ground resembled wing-back chairs. Ferns, intermingled with moss, thrived on their sturdy limbs and created a rain forest milieu.

A rooster crowed; a mother hen and her chicks dashed across the path in front of me. My eyes followed them to a calico pig snoozing under a coconut tree.

A sudden change occurred in the landscape. Jagged, black rocks intruded out the ground in a wall-like fashion. Past the natural barrier, the road climbed a hill.

Red volcanic soil replaced sand. Jungle gave way to agricultural crops. I ambled by taro swamps, pineapple fields, coconut palms, banana plants, mango and papaya trees. Unable to resist the luscious temptation that dangled overhead, I found a bamboo stalk and succeeded in whacking a papaya to the ground. It splattered on my foot. I tried again. Another effort yielded sweet victory.

"Russell, I have a papaya." He appeared.

We sat enjoying our juicy fruit on Aitu, "The Exploratory Island," a mini-archipelago in the Cook Islands, South Pacific. Nature reigns. The island has only five villages, where fewer than six-hundred residents dwell.

An international flight out of Los Angeles took us to the Cooks' main island, Raratonga; from there we flew to Atiu. Our trip took nearly two days, but prior to the airport's completion in 1978, it took much longer. It could be five weeks before a boat arrived.

Although still remote, it's easier to visit—however not many do. It's still possible to be the only tourist on the island. Since there are few visitors, those who come receive a warm welcome and special treatment.

"Greetings. So nice to have you here," Roger, the affable host of Atiu Villas said, as he extended his hand in friendship. He picked us up at the airport, and then chauffeured us to our accommodations. Along the way, he explained tidbits of the island's geology and history.

He began with Atiu's geology. Originally an underwater volcano, over eleven million years ago; it continues to rise out of the sea. Waves eroded it, while a reef grew around it. Twenty-eight sand beaches surround the shore, compliments of the erosion process. The remaining ancient coral reef—now high above the water—composed of ragged, sharp fossil coral is referred to as *makatea*. It's filled with caves and covered by jungle.

Roger then touched on the island's history. "After completion of the airport; electricity, telephone and running water followed." In 1980 a villa was built for visitors; eventually several more were added. The beautifully crafted, chalet-style cabins were constructed of available native woods.

The lodges, hand-built, featuring endemic materials, echoed the work of early Atiuians—who highly regarded carving skills. The artful masters once created bowls, drums and dug-out canoes. Today, artisans whittle storyboards—which tell a tale in pictograms—and Tangaroas, a well-endowed demigod, for tourists.

Several storyboards decorated a wall in our cottage. One portrayed the legend of the kopeka (a local bird) and two lovers in a cave. It aroused our interest. "We'll have to go find a kopeka. Rare birds," I said.

Each unit had its own private veranda, which overlooked a landscaped garden. Ours came with a friendly black-and-white cat, included at no charge. She added to our creature comforts.

A fully-equipped kitchen and well-stocked pantry greeted us. "Looks like the only eating out we need to do here is on the back porch," Russ said.

"We'll see. This place is supposed to have a gourmet cook. That sure isn't me." I didn't care much for cooking. Besides, I wasn't a good cook. Russ had known that since I fixed him a peanut butter and orange sandwich shortly after we married.

We petted our complimentary kitty. I placed my welcoming lei around her neck. She dragged it across the patio. We laughed. "I thought of a name for her, Ginger. She's a tropical delight and is good for what ails." I removed Ginger's floral necklace and we headed out.

Russ rented a scooter, the preferred form of transportation, and off we went. At certain places—due to muddy conditions—we needed to dismount to transform our "motorbike" into a "pushbike."

Most of the island we explored on our own, but heeded a local's advice to hire a guide to take us to the caves, the dwelling place of the kopekas. Marianna, our escort, led a group of us through the jungle over a narrow, crumbly pathway (the top of the *makatea*.)

"I usually hike to the caves without shoes, but today I have a sore foot," she told us, as she held up a sandaled leg.

After a strenuous, hot, uphill climb we arrived at Anataketake Cave.

Limestone overhung a gapping hole that opened into the earth. Marianna led the group down a rickety ladder; we entered the cave via a substantial opening. As our eyes adjusted to the dim light, she told us about the legendary bird.

"The kopeka, a swiftlet, is an unusual bird that nests in the darkness of this cave, and navigates about by a series of clicks." She snapped her flashlight off. The silent, damp, pitch-dark cave came to life. An eerie clicking filled the void.

"Are there any bats in there?" A tourist interrupted the unique GPS system.

"No bats live in the cave, only the birds," Marianna replied.

We lingered in the darkness for awhile, listening to the birds echo-locating.

The sound would be difficult to describe. It evoked memories of the Addams Family—Gomez, Morticia and the gang snapping their fingers—"creepy and uky."

Afterwards, Marianna asked if we'd like to follow a narrow passageway down to another cave with a pool. "Quick dip, anyone?"

A tempting offer, due to the heat and humidity; but because of my claustrophobic tendencies, I took a pass. Russ concurred. A few brave young souls forged ahead.

Spelunking completed, our guide invited us to *tumani* (bush beer school.) As we stood there with quizzical looks on our faces, she explained what it was. "Tree stumps are arranged in a circle in the jungle. Everyone sits on the log chairs, and passes around a hollowed-out coconut shell filled with local beer."

The renegade school developed when early missionaries deemed alcohol evil.

Atiuians escaped into the jungle at planned meeting places to avoid persecution.

Today the tradition continues.

I think we graduated from bush beer school, but I'm not sure. We'd been warned not to exceed ten rounds, unfortunately I lost count. I'm a notorious "lightweight." I don't believe I made it past three or four.

The last thing I recall is wandering off in a rebellious mood to climb a coconut tree—since women weren't suppose to. I later found out I climbed the wrong tree. Just as well. I'm glad I didn't offend the accommodating islanders.

The Atituians, being the gracious hosts they were, took good care of their guests. "That is one of the rules," Marianna told us. "It is your duty, to see to it that all your guests are safely returned." Great idea, otherwise there'd be lots of people traipsing about the tropical wilderness.

We found our way back to the villas, and Rodney, an internationally acclaimed chef trained in New Zealand introduced himself to us. "Hello, I'm Rodney. I will be your personal chef."

I wanted to take him home. He not only prepared great meals for us, but he'd then join us for an evening of interesting conversation afterwards.

"Well, I guess we don't have to eat every meal on the porch," Russ said, after Rodney whipped us up an epicurean delight.

"If we did, we'd be missing out. Tinned Spam couldn't hold a candle to this."

Our interest in culinary pursuits piqued, we toured a coffee farm. Free samples of Atiu coffee—which wielded a distinctive flavor—proved a savory eye-opener.

Coffee motivated us to continue our explorations, but our short time on the island had expired. "Well, guess we'd better head back and pack,' I said.

As Russ and I pulled our luggage, up the stone walkway to Roger's airport shuttle, a carefree islander bid us farewell. It still resonates with me. She invited us to, "Take a little love home." Who could resist such an offer?

CHAPTER 11

Way Down Yonder—Diving in Dixie

The lyrics of a Civil War era ballad cruised through my mind, as we sped across the sultry, northwestern segment of the Sunshine State.

"How y'all doing?" the storekeeper asked, after he'd finished putting a squat, white Styrofoam container in a 1950's era refrigerator. Russ had stopped for refreshments at a ramshackle, old-time country store. What the place lacked in luster, the clerk made up in amiability. The geriatric wood floor creaked as he approached the checkout.

I grabbed a couple of cans of lemon-lime flavored soda out of the refrigerator case, and put them on a cluttered counter. Russ couldn't resist grabbing a pepperoni stick out of the glass jar that aged by the antique cash register. "Is there gonna to be anything else today, ma'am?" the slim-jim storekeeper asked. When he leaned forward to ring up our sale, a round tin of snuff peeked out of his shirt pocket.

"No, thanks." *Ka-ching.*

"Well then, thank yah. And ma'am," he added "and have a *real* good day."

Sipping our sodas we continued on our way. At Carrabelle, large shrimp boats idled by the dock. I glanced out to sea, I saw more in sight. I couldn't seem to escape the Southern ballads; we were living them. It seemed as if we had stepped, olive drab wader first, smack dab into *Forrest Gump*.

As we cruised along the Gulf, admiring the inviting water, I wanted to get in.

"Look at all that water." I knew the plan had been to drive across the Panhandle, then head south to the Keyes to dive, but I'd flunked the Delaying Gratification 101 remedial class. "Sure would be interesting to see what's out there."

"Well, okay. I guess we can try it."

Hope this doesn't turn out to be too dumb an idea, since I suggested it, I thought.

"Hum," I uttered, as we studied the nautical chart checking depths. Ones, twos and threes stared back at us. It appeared as if someone had forgotten to finish writing a digit or two.

"Well, looks as though it may be a fairly shallow dive." I attempted to sound scholarly to add credibility to my dumb idea.

A couple of irksome inconveniences existed, sharks and alligators. We'd dived with sharks without incident. The alligators, on the other hand, represented an unknown entity. "They don't *usually* go into the Gulf. They don't like salt water," the dive shop owner had informed us. I hoped this wouldn't be an unusual dive.

Russ rented a boat and sought a dive site. Using the Loran (prior to GPS) he located a seventy-foot deep channel. We gave it a try.

The descent, into the murky depth, had no better than thirty-five-feet maximum visibility. However, the eighty-four-degree water, and calm seas, three-to-five-feet, encouraged us.

The sandy bottom revealed itself nearly devoid of life, with the exception of an assortment of sponges—including the yellow basket variety. Two-to-three-feet across they added interest to the otherwise sparse seascape.

It occurred to me that the points of intrigue would make excellent hoops. I shot a few free throws using a court-sized porifera I'd located.

Although I'll never be Air Jordan, just maybe, I'll be Water Webb.

After we returned the boat, which had been fairly expensive to rent, I suggested, "Perhaps we should wait 'til we get to the Keyes to dive."

We crossed the Ochlocknee River and continued our trek east. Placards posted along the highway urged political actions. The farther we went, the more insistent the messages became. The roadside soon became cluttered with signs: "VOTE FOR BUBBA FOR SHERIFF," "VOTE FOR CRUM FOR SCHOOL BOARD." The posters competed for space. They extended several rows deep. Most obscured the view of the next.

Russ and I stopped at a small oyster bar. Seafood, shrimp and grouper, accompanied the bivalves, as featured items. The preferred drink, sweet tea—lots of sugar, a little tea—washed the salty, sea morsels down.

Country folk surrounded us, shooting the breeze and having a good old time. Fishing stories about the one that got away, and which Crum to elect for school board, dominated animated conversations. These debates continued to grow until they reached a crescendo. Nothing appeared to have been resolved, but broad smiles conveyed the sense that most remained smug in their convictions, and enjoyed the lively discussions.

We passed through a string of small communities with unusual names. "What was that little town back there called?" I asked Russ. "Was it Porkchoppy or Slaphappy?"

"You know, I can't think of it." It would seem slightly off-kilter names should be easy to recall, but I couldn't. I rejoiced when we reached Tallahassee. I'd heard of it and could pronounce it correctly.

Tiny towns landscaped the roadside, one after another. A number of them appeared abandoned. "Maybe heat and humidity are keeping people indoors," I conjectured. Many residents that went outdoors appeared to end up at the water. The Gulf of Mexico, rivers, lakes and waterways, no doubt, offered a rejuvenating escape.

Considering the hot climate, a favorite snack seemed somewhat peculiar. The countryside had numerous signs something similar to HoT BoILeD PEaNUtS. The hand-painted sales pitches looked as though Huck Finn might have crafted them by dipping a paint brush in a bucket of black paint.

The debatable delights, as soggy as a saltine in a Gulf sugar pourer, lacked taste. Boiled in their shells, they were then laden with salt.

An acquired taste, we guessed, and preferred munch due to their widespread availability.

A great thrill occurred the day we stopped to go scalloping. In Apalachee Bay, Russ and I had the good fortune to sight a group of manatees. When the floating, docile blobs appeared, I thought they may have been the inspiration for Barney—but, they weren't purple. Gentle looking creatures, they gave the impression they wouldn't even harm a seahorse.

"Oh, look Russ. Those are the most adorable things. Well, except maybe for sea otters," I added, after I thought about it for a minute.

Sea cow sightings, considered rare, were supposed to be reported. The benign herbivores are classified as endangered. We phoned our good luck into the Manatee Hotline. Just after we called in our information, we witnessed a pod of dolphins leaping out of the water. They came to within a few feet of our boat, a real treat, although not as extraordinary as the dugong's relatives.

Our fortuitous streak didn't end with the sightings, we limited out scalloping.

Continuing on our way to Tallahassee, we made a short excursion into Georgia for dinner with relatives at a unique restaurant

The Plantation—Nicholson's Farmhouse Restaurant—proved an unforgettable experience. Part of a complex of old farmhouses, it served as a families' legacy. Passed down over several generations, the legacy fulfilled a long time dream, of opening a restaurant.

A serpentine narrow lane, shaded by centurion live oak trees curtained with Spanish moss, delivered us to the grounds. Huge blooming magnolias graced the remote location. Wild turkey preened and strutted about the grounds, wobbling their waddles.

Three structures remained from the original working farm: the main house, smokehouse and tobacco barn. Restoration had breathed new life into the possibly antebellum structures. The rich history lingered and provided wonderful, authentic touches such as wall decor of old farm implements, and daguerreotype, Victorian family portraits.

We savored a home-cooked meal, a thick steak with country biscuits and gravy, vegetables, and freshly-baked apple pie a la mode for dessert. Since beer and wine weren't served, customers bought in their own large coolers. The meal could have sated the hungriest cotton, peanut or tobacco farmer.

White tall-back, front-porch rocking chairs sat scattered on the wrap-around screened veranda. After supper, men folk made themselves comfortable on them. Ladies strolled along a path, under a tree canopy. Everything blended together to recreate the ambience of an old Southern plantation. I felt like Scarlett O'Hara that night. I imagined millinery finery atop my head, a parasol in my white lace gloves, and a fancy bustle on my fanny.

The next morning, we continued our trek south in the direction of the Florida Keys. Soon we found ourselves way down upon the Suwannee River. We continued south past Tampa, then through the Everglades to Key Largo. From there we sailed down the Overseas Highway, south toward Marathon.

"This is one big state," I commented to Russ. I'd noticed because a number of times, I'd had to turn my purse upside down and shake it, in search of coins for the toll roads.

"Imagine trying to get to the Keyes without this causeway," Russ said.

Before the completion of the across-the-ocean route, I appreciated how difficult it must have been to reach the Central Florida Keys. The islands were originally populated by tiny Key Deer, crocodiles and Indians, all of which had to swim or paddle. Now we could drive the entire length on a Sunday afternoon.

Marathon, the centrally located city of the Florida Key chain, looked like a good place to stop. A dive shop beckoned from nearly every corner. "There's another one. Let's go talk to them about going out," I said.

The owner convinced us to give the popular year-round scuba destination a try.

The morning broke sunny and warm, though a bit windy. The ocean swells ran about four-to-six-feet. The thirty-foot boat had only four divers aboard. With so few divers to watch, the captain felt comfortable attempting a deep dive on an old cable layer, the *Thunderbolt*. Sunk in one-hundred-twenty-feet of water, the shipwreck sat upright on the sandy bottom, a recent addition to the reef.

Braving the swell to escape the rocking motion of the vessel, we jumped into the water. Visibility of sixty-feet allowed us to only view half of the underwater attraction that lay on the bottom. Descending to the forward deck we observed a few spiny oysters. We continued to explore the wreck, in the fifteen minutes safely allowed at that depth. The ship remained intact, with the exception of the port holes, and precious metals removed by salvagers.

Russ pointed out a six-foot long barracuda in the wheelhouse. It startled me. The fish allowed Russ to approach within four feet. I grabbed my buddy's arm and dragged him away. I had no interest in getting up-close-and-personal with the aggressive silver scavenger.

Our time expired. Divers climbed the anchor line, stopping at ten feet to decompress. I glanced down. I could now only vaguely see the ghost-like ship beneath us. Wreck diving had never been a favorite of mine.

"That was a shipwreck," I said to Russ after spitting out my regulator.

"You're right, the *Thunderbolt*."

I'd been anxious to get to reach the Keyes. "Let's go to Key West. It's a cool place. I want to see Hemingway's six-toed cats."

"OK."

Maybe he's interested in the watermelon-pawed wonders too, I thought.

Russ and I arrived at our semitropical destination—the Southernmost City in the United States—late evening. We stepped out of the air conditioned car and into the steamy, muggy night. Live music, Jimmy Buffet genre, blasted from ubiquitous open-air eateries and taverns that lined both sides of the street.

Laughter from a clamorous restaurant lounge spilled out onto the sidewalk. Men in Havana shirts and women in flirty skirts chatted intimately. The salty sea breeze, redolent with the scents of perfume and tropical flora, captivated me. "Wow, this is pretty cool. I like it here."

"It's too touristy. I don't like it here."

"Let's go for a walk and take a look around." That lasted maybe five minutes.

"Let's go."

"But, we just got here." I knew we might as well leave. If he decided he didn't want to be there, he wouldn't be any fun anyway. We found an oceanfront hotel to spend the night.

We awoke to a perfect morning. I pulled open the drapes of our room to be enchanted by a sparkling sea. "Excellent water. We should get out and enjoy it. I can look at the cat's paws when we get home."

Russ wasn't feeling well so we decided to forgo diving. The resplendent water however, offered many opportunities, so we considered the alternatives. Russ eliminated glass bottom boats, snuba, snorkeling and dolphin tours; we'd already done those—or something more exciting.

We considered kayaking, jet skiing, or parasailing but ruled those out also. We could go fishing, but, nay, I didn't feel like that either. "I think I may be coming with something too." Neither of us could muster much enthusiasm—that meant one thing—it was time to go home.

"Interesting place, huh?" Russ said, after he returned the rental car, while we waited for the shuttle bus to take us to the airport. He seemed to perk up a little.

"Yep, I thought it had a lot of character. Wonder if they could use one more?"

Never know where we might end up next.

CHAPTER 12

Out and About in the Bahamas

I gazed out the aircraft's window dazzled by the astonishing aquascape that lay beneath us. Astronauts orbiting the earth recognized the Bahamas by the brilliant turquoise blue to shimmering emerald green hues of water.

New Providence Island, home to the capital, Nassau, where two-thirds of the population dwelled, greeted most Commonwealth of the Bahamas tourists. Our destination, however, would be the Out Islands, the more remote archipelagos.

A number of visitors flew in; many more arrived via cruise ship. Most visited Cable Beach, and then found their way across the bridge to pint-sized Paradise Island. The auxiliary isle provided a playground for well-heeled fun seekers. Luxury resorts and glitzy casinos crowded the white powder-sand beaches.

We avoided the commercialized islands and headed to the Out Islands, considered by some "in the middle of nowhere." Why? We'd discovered that each "nowhere" had its own special secrets, people and places that made for great adventures.

Johnny, our taxi driver/tour guide on Andros, epitomized one of those people. A convivial Bahamian, with a smile as wide as a piano, rushed up to greet us at the airport. He extended a welcoming hand from his short-sleeved, bright red and yellow, tropical print shirt, "Hey Mon, what's happening?" he asked, as he pumped Russ's arm.

"Let me help you with your bags," he insisted. He hauled our luggage to an antiquated, rusty, brown Buick. As he loaded it in the trunk, he announced, "This is the island I was borned on."

As we made our way to the hotel, the tropical heat and humidity caused my glasses to fog. I hastened to wipe them off, so as not to miss any of the personalized tour that Johnny provided.

Johnny told us of his love for his island. He filled us in on local information and gossip. He informed us about nearly everything we might want to, or need to know, including price of a round-trip ticket to Ft. Lauderdale ($200). It became apparent to us, if we needed anything we could ask Johnny. He would be glad to help.

He delivered us to the front steps of our hotel. Our accommodations were located on well-maintained landscaped tropical grounds, each tree trimmed and every coconut retrieved. A myriad of exotic blossoms burst forth along the walk's edge, their sweet scent filling the air.

Our room overlooked a marina adjacent to a pink-sand beach. Sago palms fringed the edge of the sparkling water, providing not only a visual delight, but shade also.

Flawless seashore beckoned. Russ and I took a stroll on a deserted beach. It seemed odd that such a paradise would be vacant. We populated the empty Eden for three heavenly days.

Since we were the hotel's only guests, we got to know the staff well. Claudette started out as our waitress, but ended up as our friend. She had just completed a six-day shift, but insisted on taking us to her favorite beach. We couldn't have found it; once off the beaten path, we became lost in the jungle.

She not only shared her island with us, but also a little about herself. Claudette grew up on Andros Island, then went to Nassau "for schooling." She didn't like it, returned home, and landed a job working at the U.S. Naval base on Andros. She worked there several years, and then decided to try something else. The hotel offered one of the few options.

Unfortunately, the weather didn't prove as hospitable as the residents. We enjoyed two good dives off Andros. Subsequently, the weather turned wretched.

Marooned onshore, by tropical thunderstorms, my buddy and I huddled together. We listened to the thunder boom louder than a steel drum whacked with a sledgehammer. We watched lighting strikes light up the dark sky brighter than a firefly at midnight. Nature provided us with an impressive show, although a disappointing one.

The poor visibility, due to the rain and fog, made it impossible to maneuver the dive boat, a good-sized trimaran, through the numerous coral heads in the shallow water. We hung out at the lodge for several hours with fellow divers, hoping it would clear. It didn't.

An island tour offered a reasonable alternative. We headed north, one of our two choices, since only one road existed, in search of a place to snorkel from shore.

Andros Town, one of the few hamlets on the island, bustled with recreational activity. Skinny hounds chased a couple of goats onto a picnic table. A few fellows fly fished. Several young scamps kicked a soccer ball around. People lingered, socializing at a family-operated five-and-ten.

The at-times adequate store had limited hours. They were closed. Open hours: 8A.M.-12A.M. and 4:00 P.M.-10:00P.M. It didn't matter anyway. Bread, milk, and other staples remained unavailable until the ferry from Nassau appeared. It arrived weekly on Tuesday. We decided to go the liquor store, which always seemed open, to get a cold drink.

We selected a couple of Kaliks (pronounced clicks) the local brew of choice. The merchant had his "church key" handy at the counter. "Would you like that opened, Mon?"

"No thanks, I'm driving," Russ said, and out we went to continue our tour.

We stopped at several nice beaches and snorkeled. The water, an inviting eighty-five degrees, made it hard to stay away. We felt the cool rain hit our backs, getting chilled briefly, but a little (or lot) of rain wasn't about to dampen our spirits.

When snorkeling, Russ happened upon an area crawling with majestic, pink-lipped queen conchs. It proved an exciting discovery to see the magnificent species thriving.

Conch proved ubiquitous in the Bahamas. Almost every restaurant and bar in the islands featured two items: conch and grouper. I can attest they are as tasty as they are beautiful.

The rawness of Andros, an unpopulated wild place, made it a first-class destination to explore. It is by far the largest of the seven-hundred islands, and more than two-thousand cays (pronounced keys) that make up the island chain of the Bahamas. Much of the island remains inaccessible, covered by thick, dense jungle brush. Getting to the beach can be challenging due to the limited access.

Few visitors find their way there. Sailors might arrive via their private yachts out of Florida. Scuba divers could wander by, knowing Andros boosts the third longest reef in the world. Other adventurers may include sport anglers who come to partake in world-class fishing.

Yachtsmen tend to stay aboard, only wandering onshore at sunset for a Planters Punch or Gombay Smash at a nearby beach bar. Enjoyable, no doubt, however Andros had much more to offer. The legendary, mischievous *chickcharnies*—elfin-like creatures that dwell in forests, capable of granting life-long luck—didn't even have to hide the pleasures of their island. Many visitors simply didn't seek them.

Time got away from us faster than a speeding barracuda. I packed our soggy bags and we headed to Nassau for a day, en route to Eleuthera.

Nassau proved a striking contrast to the island we'd left, as tame as Andros was wild.

Tourist activities included: Coral World, a huge aquarium pumping

50,000 gallons of sea water through every hour; Cable Beach, a premier resort area filled with luxury hotels and restaurants; the Straw Market, a bit of Bahamian culture parked in tiny stalls, filled with items of almost every description; and Atlantis Resort and Casino that sits on a fourteen-acre waterscape, with six lagoons on the beach.

I'd liked to have stayed longer. We had time to enjoy a yummy breakfast, Johnny cakes and grits at Cable Beach, and do a little shopping.

"Isn't this delicious?"

Russ looked at me like I'd spent too much time in the sun.

We made a quick stop at the Straw Market, just long enough for two local ladies to turn me into a Bahama Mama. They braided my hair and tied a bright purple fringed wrap skirt, adorned with seashells and star fish, around my waist. The islanders tried to turn Russ into a Bahama Papa, but he didn't want his hair braided. The women tried to convince him, he had enough (hair that is). He decided on a T-shirt instead. The merchants giggled and chattered as they dug through a tall, leaning stack of shirts to find his size.

After having a great time at the Straw Market (well I did anyway), we scurried, getting drenched, to the Atlantis Resort.

The resort, turned out to be a mind-boggling place. Activity defined its essence. I suspected it impossible to do everything.

The grounds featured a huge underground aquarium, a live reggae band playing beside the water-park, dolphins leaping through hoops in a pool, a jet-ski and parasailing area just off the beach.

Numerous activities included golf, shopping, charters and a spa.

Entertainment abounded. A casino, restaurants, theater, bars, and lounges littered the hotel.

We were amused by the dolphins and ogled the sharks in the aquarium. "That's a good place for them," I noted.

I wandered into the casino and lost a couple of rolls of quarters. My luck in the casino was no better than our luck with the weather.

The atmospheric conditions, almost anyone that lives here can tell you—are always a gamble.

"Is this weather typical?" I asked the ticket agent at the airport.

"No, Sue," he said, after reading my name on the ticket. "I promise you, the sun will come out tomorrow." Off we went chasing our pot of gold, and hoping he was right.

Eleuthera is derived from the Greek word for freedom. It seemed an appropriate place to spend Independence Day. To us it meant freedom from foul weather. A few days began with thunderstorms, and a few ended with them, but there wasn't a day we didn't see the sun for awhile.

We didn't do much diving. Hundreds of miles of accessible, sandy beaches to discover and snorkel welcomed us; unlike on Andros, where lack of roads hampered access. Sticking to shore explorations enabled us to save considerable cash.

The Queen's Highway, a passable thoroughfare, stretched the length of the island. The road, constructed of thin pavement, sat atop the coral foundation. It proved an excellent breeding ground for potholes and made for jumpy journeys. Her Majesty would be in dismay if she witnessed the behavior of her royal subjects on her road. Nevertheless, it paved the way to adventure.

Road signs eluded us. They were knocked down, too weather-worn to read, placed too high to notice, or oddly abbreviated making them unintelligible.

If, we stopped to ask locals for directions they were apt to tell us, "Turn at the green dumpster." Unfortunately dumpsters move. Even worse, "Turn at the church." There must be almost as many churches on Eleuthera, as there were grains of sand.

We thought getting around would be "…a cinch" since there was only one main route. However, to get to the beaches, we had to detour from it, and then guess which of many smaller lanes to choose.

Small paths narrowed until often snuffed out by tropical vegetation. At times we found ourselves on someone's driveway, ending up at a tropical fruit farm. Private drives led to off-shore owned expensive estates. Each had its own name emblazoned in script on a brass plaque, hidden away behind a burglar-proof, ornate, black wrought-iron gate.

"I want one of those," I said to Russ, as we were turning around in a professionally landscaped drive. "I'm going to call it, Suzy's Scuba Shack."

"Isn't that a simple name for such a fancy home?"

"I'm a simple person."

Not many residents seemed to own motor vehicles. They either walked or rode bicycles. On Saturdays a favorite recreation seemed to be piling as many people as possible in one of the few cars.

Her majesty's highway became a bumpy collision course. Jockeying for space got competitive. I supplied the play-by-play for Russ of the POTHOLES 500 (five-hundred potholes) in my NASCAR announcer's voice.

"A seasoned taxi driver takes the lead. A rental car driver, not too concerned about the fate of his vehicle comes up fast from behind. Whoa—looks like, yes, he went flying through that car-swallowing pothole. Off to the far right a middle-aged man, maneuvers his old and rusty, but highly-valued Chevy, through a well-rehearsed routine. Obviously, he's done that before, Russ. Meanwhile, a young rookie, with reggae music blasting, approaches from behind. He overtakes the pack and grabs the lead."

The entire drag became blocked with cars, like ants having a field day at a picnic. As the day wore on, the traffic dissipated, the excitement waned, and life returned to its slow, relaxed pace.

"Wow, what an adrenaline rush! You should be qualified for Le Mans now," I said, only partially joking.

Racing thrills aside, we heard the call of the sea. We weren't sure which one though—the Atlantic or the Caribbean, both lingered within a couple of miles' distance.

Russ and I tore ourselves away from the water to eat. At Lower

Brogue, Mrs. B's Lifesaver and Take Away Restaurant caught our eye. The ambitious enterprise was governed by Beulah, who wore all the hats. Her little café featured cozy round tables covered with red-checkered tablecloths. On each sat a bud vase with a single artificial flower. Displayed prominently on the wall hung a sign: I FIGHT PROVERTY, I WORK.

Mrs. B dished us up warm hospitality along with a gourmet-prepared crawfish (lobster) dinner. She artfully mastered the skill of blending herbs and spices to tantalize almost every taste bud in a different manner. It proved nothing short of world-class.

As she served us dinner, she shared her life. She, currently a justice of peace, had thrown one of her many hats in the ring for mayor. The election date, July 26th approached. "If I could vote for her I would. I bet she'd always be cooking up something good," I said.

She insisted we return the following evening for dinner. She would specially prepare anything we wished. We had grown tired of the standard hotel offering of conch and grouper. We accepted her generous offer and placed our order for the next evening. Lobster, peas & rice, beans & grits (a couple of local favorites) with guava duff for dessert.

The next day we returned with worthy appetites. We'd spent the day snorkeling and swimming. Perhaps our hunger enhanced the tastiness, but again Mrs. B dished up outstanding fare—except for dessert. Guava duff is the poi of desserts; a good way to ruin a great meal. Yet we appreciated her effort.

Russ and I rose early the next morning for a trip to Harbour Island, a ten-minute boat ride. Water taxis (local's old fishing boats) waited at the docks to transport tourists to and fro.

The dive shop for the area was situated on the island, a far more tourist-oriented place. We intended to have breakfast at the nearby open-air marina, but after hearing a group of divers ask the waitress, "Do you suppose it might be possible to get some toast in forty-five minutes?" we decided to forgo breakfast.

Russ rented a couple of tanks for a shore dive, then had the dive master radio back across the channel, for a water taxi to pick us up later.

The aquatic paradise, once again, didn't fail to please. Fish, bright and colorful, flitted about. One small fry, with a neon-orange head and electric blue tail, joined us. He turned out to be a pleasant companion—good as a puppy.

Star shells lay strewn about on the limestone shore. Lustrous light shone on the clear water, creating delicate filigree that penetrated the surface, and highlighted the beautiful underwater environs. I found myself thinking, *I wish I could stay here forever*.

The days slipped away. The time arrived to return home. I tried to take a mental snapshot of our last day, the early morning swim and walk on the beach.

When I think of the Bahamas, I, like the astronauts, will remember it for the water. No matter what the perspective, a celestial or terrestrial one, the water is unforgettable.

I now knew the best reason to go to the Out Islands, in the middle of nowhere. Nowhere, is there a better place to be.

CHAPTER 13

Palau and Chuuk, Micronesia—Pow, Ow

Screech—POW!! We spun around three-hundred-sixty degrees. Sunglasses flew from my face. My head impacted the back of the seat. It happened so fast, yet it felt as though it happened in slow motion. I sat dazed, staring straight ahead.

Just moments ago, on the last leg of our grueling trip to Palau—a short sojourn in Guam—we'd gulped down a cup of coffee, then hurried to the lobby, to catch the airport shuttle.

The shuttle driver, running late, pulled out in front of a small car. The little vehicle packed a big wallop. It smashed into the van, outside the window where Russ and I sat.

"Are you okay?" Russ asked, as he fumbled for his cell phone to call 911.

"I think so." I felt warm blood trickling down my cheek.

The shrill sound of sirens approaching broached my daze. Paramedics loaded me into the ambulance. *Things like this aren't supposed to happen on vacation*, I thought.

Russ came out of the accident unscathed. I received a nasty cut above my left eye. Getting painful stitches in the Guam Hospital concluded the sad incident.

Discharged after several hours, I recuperated quickly, but got the bad news. Scuba diving, or even snorkeling, would be verboten until the stitches were removed.

Like E.T., I wanted to go home. We called our travel agent in Portland. She contacted the booking company to get us an earlier flight. "No dice."

Our agent then tried the local airline in Guam, to explain our situation and get us replacement tickets. "Oh, yes. I passed the accident on the way to work this morning," the ticket agent recalled. She had us on the next flight.

Our Micronesian odyssey entailed a complicated itinerary. The flight out of Los Angeles landed us in Guam, Micronesia's hub, where the accident occurred.

From there we flew to Palau where our expedition began. The Republic of Palau consisted of two groups: the Palau Islands and the South-West Islands. We would be visiting three of the five main archipelagos: Babeldaod, Koror, Peleli and the Rock Islands. The final jaunt of our involved itinerary: Chuuk, aka Truk.

Babeldaob Island began the Republic of Palau segment. The K-B Bridge connected Babeldoab to Koror. We taxied from the airport on Babeldaob to our hotel on Koror. From Koror, we traveled to the Rock Islands and Peleliu.

After touring Peleliu we returned to Koror. We then taxied back to Babeldaob to return to Guam; from there we flew to Chuuk.

Chuuk completed, we again returned to Guam to fly home.

I remained rattled; the entire trip seemed somewhat surreal. The complexity of our itinerary further exaggerated my befuddlement. I harbored a vague sense of disorientation. Russ made sure we were at the right place, at the right time.

Babeldaob, the largest island in the Palau group, had only a handful of roads, except near the south end by the airport. The lack of roads presented difficulties. Limited shore access prohibited snorkeling and diving.

Russ and I tried the next island.

Koror, the most populated island, the capital and economic heart of the Palau group, wasn't the idyllic picture of a palm-covered sandy paradise. Few beaches existed. Mangroves cluttered the shores.

Our hotel on Koror Island had a splendid view of delightful water on one side, and the municipal dump on the other.

What a stinking vacation this is turning out to be, I thought.

My buddy and I tried the next islands.

The Rock Islands, the smallest in the lagoon, exhibited the true beauty of Palau. They appeared to be the paradise we sought. An aquatic wonderland—and I couldn't go into the water.

As I gazed upon the splendiferous sea, I pondered the wonderful opportunities we had been given. As a diver, I didn't have to admire things from a distance. I could experience nature intimately and interact with it.

The islets resembled lush, emerald-green toadstools as they thrust out of the cerulean lagoon water. Each land mass originated from of a piece of ancient coral reef, which had turned to limestone, and then been pushed out of the water. Unusual sights, they were unlike anything we'd seen in our travels.

Some soared into the air fifty feet or more. A dense jungle of trees, bushes and vines covered most of them. Water had eroded many of their bases, as much as ten feet in places, giving them an umbrella-like appearance

The mushroom-like protrusions varied in size from several acres to a few feet. A smattering of the larger ones had beaches. Countless numbers of them crowded the ocean. I tried counting them, but lost track.

"Cloud Cove," the captain yelled. The skipper bought the boat to a halt. "We'll be stopping here to snorkel."

The snorkelers jumped off the boat. After they began exploring, I figured out how the site got its name.

The underwater cave, inside a rock wall, had a large air pocket at the end where fog formed.

"This is a blast," Russ shouted up to me. I watched him rollick. He entered by swimming into the submerged tunnel. He bobbed up and down with the surge, which rushed in and out of the opening.

I wasn't the only one watching Russell play in the cave. A squid also took notice. Russ went down, the squid went up. Russ went up, the squid went down. I don't know if it was a coincidence, or the squid actions were intentional, but he inversely mimicked my husband's every move. The cephalopod cracked me up.

"What's so funny?" Russ wondered, upon one of his cave exits.

"That darn squid—he's like a piston. He's mirroring your actions in reverse. It's hilarious." I longed to join him. I wanted to play too.

The clarity of the water made it possible to see to the bottom. In the shallows of the lagoon; colorful, three-feet-long, giant tridacna clams, lay visible on the bottom. I became intrigued by their beauty and sought out more information.

Like sea turtles, these clams are now protected by Palauan law. However, since the demand for clam meat still exists, the government built a clam farm on Koror.

Russ and I visited it. The clam farmers appreciated our interest and gave us a tour.

"We have eight varieties of clams. The smaller species we raise for their shells. The meat is tough and not good to eat," an aquaculturist informed us. One clam measured about a foot in length. We wondered how long it took to grow. "About eight years," the farmer estimated.

Eventually, the clams were harvested and sold to Japanese restaurants. I tried one at a local oriental eatery. I gnawed on it until I felt like a cow with cud.

"Chewy, huh?" Too busy grinding to answer, Russ just grinned.

We purchased a tridacna shell from the farm. Cultured shells were allowed to be brought back through customs. It entailed a bit of red tape. Russ paid two dollars for a permit, and then waited four hours for the Palauan Fish and Game Minister to sign it. "Good things come to those who wait. Guess giant clam shells are good things," I noted.

After securing our purchase, we set sail to Peleliu, a small island in the Republic of Palau. It lay just south of the Rock Islands.

Considered one of the finest underwater drop-offs in the world, the Peleliu Wall awaited. It quickly drops from ten-feet to over nine-hundred-feet. Excited about making the dive, Russ grabbed the first available opening.

Divers suited up, and hit the water. They descended to one-hundred-feet then rose up the wall. Corals, hard and soft, and sponges covered it. At about thirty-feet, the wall crested and the current increased.

"I had to hold on tight. The current rushing by felt like a like a fire hydrant having the pressure released." Russ said. He couldn't turn his head or his mask would be ripped off. He'd anchored himself, with a large hook, cord attached—at the advice of a friend who dove it—to a dead coral head. There he and the other divers waited.

In a short time, the divers were surrounded, in front and along side, by sharks—black-tips, white-tips and gray reef. The predators hung around to feast on fish that came up over the edge of the wall. Behind them, hundreds of schooling barracudas treaded water. The scavengers bided their time awaiting any leftover morsels.

Russ beamed as he climbed back on board. He couldn't wait to relate his story. "If I stared straight ahead into the current, the sharks would come in closer. If I held my mask on, and turned to look at them, they'd back away." He dropped his weight belt, took off his mask and began unbuckling his fins. He hadn't finished doffing his gear before he started gushing.

"Great dive! Fantastic! Probably one of the most memorable I've ever made." Russ, unusually buoyed, summarized the experience. He didn't impress easily, having logged four-hundred-nineteen prior dives.

"Darn," I said, not wanting to spoil his excitement. *Was I ever lucky to have missed that one*, I thought. Maybe everything really did happen for a reason.

After Russ made the dive on the Peleliu Wall, we returned to Guam. Our next and last destination would be Weno Island, Chuuk's capital and business center.

While in Guam, I had my stitches removed. "Yippee, stitch free! I anticipate our trip to Chuuk with elation; I'd soon be able to again enjoy participation." My exuberance at being able to return to the water inspired poetry, bad poetry.

The departing plane appeared to have few passengers. Its primary purpose, rather, seemed to be the transport of cargo. The majority of people wielded ice chests and boxes they pushed along on luggage carts. They nudged bulkier items forward with their feet, as the check-in line advanced.

Parcels of nearly every size and description crowded the boarding area. Some items were tied with twine, a few held together by duct tape, most scribbled on with a black felt-tip marker. The freight mandated the flight loaded at the cargo terminal, rather than the passenger terminal.

The only thing this hodgepodge had in common—their destination. Chuukies shopped in Guam, and then shipped the merchandise back home.

Flying into Chuuk, I noticed housing cluttered the shoreline, while tropical rainforests covered the interior. To further get our bearings, once on the ground, we took a tour.

Henry, an affable young man, drove us around in his SUV. He delivered us to the bank, to exchange traveler's checks. Russ went in, while I waited with Henry. Russ spent at least forty-five minutes in the financial facility. We happened to get there during open hours—there weren't many.

"That's my brother. He takes divers out on the boat," Henry said, pointing out a young man across the parking lot, who looked nothing like him. "Half-brother," he added.

An older woman leaned in the open passenger-side window, resting her arms on the door, "How ya doing Henry?' she asked.

"Just fine." He turned to look at me, "That's my aunt."

As soon as she left, a steady stream of people stopped by the car window, as if queuing up at a ticket box office. Each one greeted him; they were either relatives of Henry's, or friends of Henry's. I'm convinced he knew almost everyone in town.

"What's up with Chuuk?" I asked. "Why does this island seem to have two different names?" I'd noted that most of the signs in town said Truk.

"Truk," he said, "means nothing. Chuuk means mountains. The islands in the lagoon were named after their tall peaks. Germans occupied the islands during the war. They had difficulty pronouncing Chuuk. When they tried, it sounded like Truk, so it became Truk."

I had to laugh when I asked for a good place to eat, "Try the Truk Stop Restaurant, good food," Henry advised.

Russ and I stayed at the Truk Continental Hotel located by a sandy beach with a lagoon view. A good choice since most of the waterfront, private land, prohibited accessibility. Residents tended to view the beaches behind their homes as their private fishing grounds. Diving interested us more anyway.

The wrecks of the Truk Lagoon were rumored among the finest in the world. The World War II artifacts remained accessible, although protected. Nothing could be removed and thus remained well-preserved. Divers from around the world came to explore the relics in the Truk lagoon. It brimmed with Japanese ships sunk in Operation Hailstorm.

Our first morning in the hotel's dining room we met a group of middle-aged British divers who specialized in WWII shipwrecks. Their neglected breakfasts and half-full coffee cups had been pushed aside in favor of enormous nautical charts that covered several tables. "What do you say? We start here, explore it thoroughly, and have enough bottom time left to safely make that," he said pointing at another part of the chart, "our second dive."

We chatted with them briefly. They had a detailed analysis and the technical specifications for every wreck in the lagoon. It astounded me. I became curious about where they gained their expertise. "Books. Lots of books about these you know." It seems there's a cottage industry on Truk lagoon shipwrecks.

Russ and I dove four: the *Fujikawa Maru*, the *Yamagiri Maru*, the *Shinoku Maru* and the *Sankisan Maru*. (*Maru* is Japanese for ship.)

The depth of the dives averaged one-hundred-feet. The deep wrecks served as artificial reefs, enveloped by soft and hard corals. Colorful delights, Russ' dive light dive light revealed a panorama of hues, we later saw in his flash photos.

My buddy and I swam around the decks and upper hold areas, the bottom often being too deep to safely approach. The holds harbored airplanes, engines, jeeps, tanks, ammunition, hardware, and other reminders of the raging conflict. Assorted relics of everyday life lay about, ranging from china to sake bottles.

The evidence of how they sunk I found most intriguing. The aftermath of the siege, as they went down in history remained readily apparent—torpedo holes and missing halves. "I bet those British divers could tell us what fired the torpedo that made that gaping hole, and what happened to the other end of that ship," I said.

"I'm sure they could."

Sated with wreck-diving, I chartered a small boat to go snorkeling at the lagoon's edge. I recognized the boat's driver immediately—Henry's brother. "Good morning." He had a genial smile. "Ready to go?"

"Rip-roaring ready," I replied "Let's go!"

A number of *motus*—uninhabited small islands—lay scattered in the pristine water. Palm trees fluttered in the breeze on some; others had no vegetation.

Sparkling sunlight infiltrated the salty expanse. Fish at abysmal depths were visible. The marine environment evoked memories of the Rock Islands.

At the edge of the lagoon, our guide stopped at a half-acre white-sand *motu*. On the lonely beach stood a single room structure, built on three-foot-high stilts. It could be rented for the night. Underneath the room, a bucket sat chock-full with baby sea turtles.

"I'm going to let them go," a young scamp told us. I hoped he did.

Russ and I stumbled upon a stone fire pit filled with ashes. Conch shells lay strewn about. Hundreds of shells blanketed the shore. "Now I know why these are called picnic islands," I said.

My buddy and I snorkeled in water two or three feet deep. Patches of coral, embedded in fine white sand, highlighted our swim. I kicked back, floating with my face to the sun. Fish flittered around. I lazily surfed the occasional boat wakes that washed by. *I can't imagine a much more perfect life*, I thought.

Henry's half-brother, who napped while we explored, awoke. "Hey!" He stuck a couple of fingers in his mouth and whistled loud, then made a sweeping motion for us to return.

Russ signed our names, along with other visitors, to the side of a log with ashes from the fire. I began gathering our things.

After stowing our snorkel gear in large goody bags, we slung them over our shoulders and walked hand-in-hand across the sand.

Wading through the shallow water to the waiting boat, I reflected on our unexpected journey. I realized, no matter how many plans a person may make—what will unfold is beyond their control.

CHAPTER 14

Tobago—Close Encounters with the Robinsons

As a wayward cow slogged through the duck's pond, an agitated hen scurried to chase her fuzzy ducklings out of harm's way. The drake observed from his perch atop a tree branch. Several other ducks floated languidly along, unperturbed by the commotion. Two snowy white egrets loitered alongside a long forgotten water wheel, covered in vine and frozen in time.

Russ and I stood in front of the Speyside hotel, across the gravel road from the small body of water, watching the events unfold. First impressions led us to believe we'd witnessed the excitement for the day. Boy, were we ever wrong!

Tobago, where Speyside is located, sits above her larger sister island, Trinidad, off the coast of Venezuela in the southern Caribbean Sea.

Trinidad embodies the quintessential Caribbean island, famous for Carnival and Calypso; she tends to overpower her little sibling. Tobago offers the same revelries, but on a scaled back level. The ambience is more akin to a small town than a large city.

We looked around the grounds, and then checked in. Russ noticed that a crucial piece of luggage had vanished. It contained our scuba gear. Another bit of bad luck. Diving proved impossible anyway, the weather wasn't co-operating. My buddy and I considered other possibilities.

After registering, we opted to take a ride. Russ secured a rental vehicle, and off we went.

After we'd been on the road for awhile, refreshments seemed like a good idea. Russ pulled over at a roadside fruit stand.

"Hey, Mon—would you like to try my *special* drink?" asked the dread-locked vendor, sporting a cap knitted in the colors of the Ethiopian flag. "It's got fresh coconut milk, carrots and bananas." He paused. "My friend," he said to Russ, "If you drink this, you'll give the ladies problems."

"Think I may have enough problems. Thanks though."

The salesman responded with a sly smile and a wink. "Well, if you don't like it today, maybe you'll like it tomorrow. Come back then."

My buddy and I continued on our trek. Driving around Tobago shouldn't take that long, I figured. The island measured twenty-six miles long and three miles wide. Until we'd driven the length of it, I had no idea how long that distance could be.

The circular route began in Speyside, a small town that served as the scuba diving center. It meandered precariously through villages, terminating on the other side of the island at Scarborough. Hairpin turns tighter than knots, folded one upon another. The highway hugged a steep hillside, no shoulder, no guardrail, only a sheer drop to the ocean below.

School children, attired in crisp plaid uniforms, stood brazenly in the narrow road, with their thumbs up, looking for a ride to school. "Roxborough!" They yelled their desired destination to us as we passed, hoping we'd pick them up.

Vehicular traffic and pedestrians weren't the only ones utilizing the crowded roadway. Cattle roamed the thoroughfare; chickens dashed about.

The busy byway also served as a social center for chatty residents.

In several areas the congested, hair-raising route slid toward the sea, requiring the use of makeshift detours.

Russ determined it best to drive as little as possible. The undeniable urge to explore, however, compelled us to wander.

"Do you think I can make it?" Russ foolishly asked. Anyone who knew me would think he'd have known better.

I jumped out to take a look down the crossroad, just itching to go see what lingered off the beaten path.

"Oh, heck yes. You're not going to have any trouble."

Russ followed a cow trail-like, side road down a steep, grassy hillside. The lane rambled about on a cliffside that dropped off into the ocean. It took no time to get to the bottom. We had gravity working to our advantage.

The sky darkened and rain loomed. "Looks like it might rain. Maybe we should head back," I said.

As Russ looked for a place to turn around, a torrential downpour washed all such thoughts from his mind. Within ten minutes our bovine pathway had been refashioned into a slick mud slide. We weren't going anywhere.

Russ and I would have to rely on our on ingenuity to save us—somewhat of an iffy proposition in my case. No cell phone service existed and it seemed unlikely that someone else might pass by.

"Let's see if we can get this thing going." Russ jammed his foot down hard on the accelerator. The jeep-like, small SUV revved, the wheels spun, but there was no forward motion. He tried again. It yielded the same result.

"You steer, I'm going to get out and push."

I got behind the wheel. He went to the back of the vehicle.

"Okay, hit it." The mud flew.

"Hit it again." The mud flew higher.

The baby off-roader skated around on the mud like an ice dancer, but refused to go up the hill. Soon Russ was covered in mud and mad as a hornet. He resembled a Papua New Guinea Mudman. When I glanced back, all I could see were the whites of his eyes.

I knew I had to choose my words judiciously. "I think we may be getting stucker."

He walked to the front and said nothing. He didn't need to, I knew *basically* the fault lay with me, but, I wasn't the one driving.

"Let's go for a walk and think about this," I suggested. The walk proved to be a hike through dense jungle, which ended up at the beach. The temperature lingered around one-hundred degrees. "It'll be cooler by the water." I hoped.

The rain left as quickly as it had come. The sun began to break through the clouds. As we approached the ocean, we could see the sun shining on the shore.

"What a beautiful beach. Just think, if we hadn't gotten stuck, we probably would never have found this." I realized I sounded a little like Pollyanna.

He didn't say anything—he still wasn't talking to me.

Pondering our fate, we sat quietly on the beach watching the waves break.

If a perfect beach existed, this had to be it. The land curved around forming a horseshoe-shaped inlet. High cliffs dropped down to kiss the sand. Tropical vegetation decorated the cliffs, while exposed roots accessorized the sheer drops. Fine, pale, cherry-blossom pink sand greeted the light, emerald-blue water.

As I sat there, in silence, I had a sense of déja vu. The Swiss Family Robinson, a favorite film from my childhood, was filmed on Tobago. I wondered if they shot footage on this beach, and that's why it seems as though I've seen it before.

Sitting there, I felt like a Robinson or a shipwrecked stowaway who washed up on the shore. Just me and the sea—it didn't take too much imagination.

I experienced a kinship with nature similar to the type I feel when I'm scuba diving, an intimate connection to the planet.

We sat on the beach for quite awhile. Shadows began to fall and convinced us we needed return.

While schlepping back across the deserted beach, I found a tangled fishing net, half-buried in the sand. "Traction! Maybe we could put it under the tires and use it like chains." The seine might hold my redemption.

Deep in the sand, it proved difficult to extract, but Russ had a pocketknife. He hacked at the knotted, green twine. After a great deal of effort he extricated it.

I dragged it across the sand and back into the jungle.

By the time we returned to the road, it had dried it out somewhat.

"Well, what do you think?" I asked Russ.

He accessed our predicament. "I've got an idea."

He always did. No matter how dire the situation I found myself in, he saved me. I've lost track of how many times.

"This is what we'll do. See that hillside over there?" A cuesta loomed beside us. "There's some dry soil underneath the overhang. Grab the tire iron. We'll use it to chip away some dry earth and rebuild the road."

Well, there's something I'd never done on vacation before—build a road.

Russ and I excavated the dry dirt. Russ put it over the mud, around the tires. Then I shoved the net in front of the tires, so once they started to move we'd continue to have traction. "Now, that's what I call teamwork," I said.

"Better than most of the roads of the island," I said, admiring our work.

Russ got in and put the petal-to-the-metal. Several attempts yielded only frustrating failures. The stubborn off-road vehicle finally lurched forward. We were freed. Rarely had I'd ever been so thankful.

We'd planned our vacation to coincide with Russ' birthday. The day we got stuck happened to be that day. "Your 40th should be a memorable day. Bet you'll never forget this one."

"You're right about that."

Little did Russ know, his surprises for the day weren't over quite yet.

My buddy and I headed back to the hotel for dinner. I'd made arrangements with two friendly hotel employees to surprise him. They delighted in conspiring with me. "But we don't have any birthday cakes," one of the ladies informed me.

Local baked goods tended to reflect the bounty of the island: coconut sweetbread, cassava pone or perhaps a fruitcake, made of tropical fruit.

One of the quick-witted gracious ladies, who were beyond accommodative, came up with an idea. "We have some peanut butter, flour and sugar—we will try and make one."

The birthday boy and I enjoyed a tasty meal of curried crab 'n dumplings washed down with a ginger beer. *Wonder if we might be having peanut butter cake for dessert?*

Fresh seafood specialties abounded due to the proximity of the sea and rivers: grouper, crab, lobster, conch, mahi mahi, red snapper, shrimp, oysters and crayfish were among the myriad of choices.

On the island, Creole style—highly seasoned dishes—reigned as the preferred preparation. Normally I couldn't wait for the next meal. Today, however, I couldn't wait to finish dinner and surprise Russ.

"*Happy Birthday to you...*" floated out of the kitchen, as the swinging doors opened and my two co-conspirators entered the dining room. One held a light brown cake. A single candle flickered on top.

The ladies approached the table. One placed the cake directly in front of Russ, and the other gave him a peck on the cheek. He again sat speechless, but this time in a good way. I knew his 40th he would never forget.

The next day we received some good news. The lost luggage containing our scuba gear had been found. Off we went to Roxborough to retrieve it.

On our mission we noticed a road sign, Robinson Crusoe's Cave. "Let's stop. I'm curious about it." I said.

Russ parked in a sandy lot. A guide met us and took us the short distance, down a path, to the water's edge. "There it is," he said pointing to the opening, after collecting his fee.

We gazed into the escarpment to see a hole-in-the-wall, carved out perhaps by wave action. It appeared too small for a dwelling, but large enough for a tourist trap.

"Our close encounter with the other Robinsons was a lot more interesting," I said. Disappointed, but probably wiser, we continued on our way to the airport.

After picking up our luggage, it remained too early to call it a day. We continued exploring the island, not detouring far from the main road. Russ made one exception and attempted a trip into the mountainous interior.

Russ and I had planned to hike in the Tobago Forest Reserve. A farsighted individual set it aside as a reserve in 1765, an area of unspoiled tropical beauty; however it became spoiled for us.

As Russ parked, an employee of the Trinidad and Tobago tourist bureau warned us it wasn't safe to go hiking without a guide. A problem existed. Drug addicts on dirt bikes tore out of the surrounding forest, and robbed tourists of their belongings and clothes. That could be ugly.

"Forget hiking. Let's go diving instead," I suggested. We now had our gear and the weather had calmed down. Good decision.

The diving quite literally swept us off our feet. My buddy and I were carried along by the current. We flew past brain corals, French angels, parrot fish, trigger fish, butterfly fish, snappers, groupers, rays, and turtles. I tried not to focus on anything too long, afraid I'd miss something else. Russ and I were participants in a moving diorama. We advanced through it much too quickly. The dive provided an array of sights—and an exciting ride.

Diving wasn't the only thing that provided a lively show on Tobago. "The pulling of the net," also did. This lively tradition gathered men from surrounding villages, who cast a seine over a small bay adjacent to their communities. Slow and steady, exerting strenuous effort, they hand-over-hand pulled the net in. Their bulging muscles testimony to their powerful labor, their strong arms and upper torsos glistened in the sun, as the net neared the shore.

The villagers developed a rhythm, all working together to accomplish their common goal. They continued pulling, bringing the net closer and closer together, as it neared the shore. Finally their exhausting teamwork paid off as they pulled the net up on the shore. Any fish were then equally divided. The process seemed at least as important as the outcome.

As our time on Tobago drew to a close, I reflected on our visit. I learned the value of creativity, optimism, resourcefulness, teamwork, and road construction.

Russ and I had many paths left to explore. We'd see where they took us, and if we had to build them.

CHAPTER 15

Solomon Islands—Diving and Drifting in Time

Smoke spiraled out of the dirt floor, thatched dwelling. A friendly Melanesian woman poked her head out an opening and invited us in. A pot boiled; steam poured off. The palm frond ceiling had been charred black by the stone fire pit. A chicken pecked at a piece of coconut meat that lay discarded in the cooking area.

Later, we stood in the Solomon Islands National Museum, viewing photographs taken over one-hundred years ago, by a London adventurer. One-thousand remote islands in the South Pacific remained virtually unchanged since the Royal Geographical Society had visited them more than a century earlier.

Saeraghi Village, a traditional settlement that mirrored the museum dioramas, contained sixty-five homes. About seventy-five percent of the people dwell in rural areas. Their residences, constructed of sago-palm thatching, featured food preparation and sleeping areas. The abodes, many on stilts, had apertures from which to take advantage of the sea breeze.

As the villager stirred the pot, she spoke in Pidgin English. Nearly half the population did. The simplified language allowed two groups who didn't share a common language, to communicate. She conversed in a rapid manner, stopping occasionally for us to respond. We listened to her, smiled and nodded, not understanding a word she said.

This village, like many others, nestled up to the coast line in proximity to freshwater springs. Islanders, for the most part, made their livings farming and fishing. Families owned coconut plantations and vegetable plots. Traditional crops, such as taro, were grown in shared village areas.

Vivid colors defined the hamlets. "We call those Christmas flower trees," the woman replied when we asked about the brilliant, blooming red trees.

"Can you do a twirly for me?" The prismatic parrot spun around at his owner's beseeches. As he twirled, he talked. He also spoke Pidgin. We didn't understand him either.

A calico pig rooted, as drool dribbled out of his mouth. He wallowed in a pen made of cane secured with hemp, tethered to wooden stakes. He wiled away the hours until the day came he would go to market.

Village women tended the market—the hamlet's core—in its daily operations beside the harbor. They displayed bananas, coconuts, limes, watermelons, sweet potatoes and breadfruit on a series of long weather-worn tables. A jumble of seashells added variety and contrast.

Activity defined the market. Fibrous husks flew as women handled the difficult task of opening coconuts. The women, attired in tropical garb, mingled and laughed. Purchasers chatted, bargained and feigned shock at asking prices. After sufficient negotiation, buyer and seller concurred, all in a good-natured manner.

Men fished daily in dug-out canoes. If successful, they'd bring in tuna and reef fish. They displayed their catch on woven mats adjacent to the dusty road, in hopes of a sale. The angler-merchants waved palm fronds to keep the flies away, while splashing water on their catch to keep it fresh. "Hey, don't step on my fish," the fishmonger yelled at the kids as they scurried by.

A passel of youngsters chased one another around the market, and then scampered off to the docks. With flying leaps they launched into the warm water. Squealing with delight, they'd climb out, then run back and do it again.

The weather suddenly changed. The azure sky darkened as a thunderbolt struck, igniting a tropical downpour. People continued about their business unfazed. A few older women popped up brightly colored umbrellas. The children seemed to be further energized, running faster and jumping higher off the old pier.

While we enjoyed the opportunity to glimpse into the traditional life of the Solomon Islanders, we hadn't seen anything yet. We were about to embark on a journey to one of the eeriest places we'd ever been privy to, Skull Island.

Chief Eddie flashed a big grin as he waded out to the boat. A slight man, his dignity exceeded his physical stature. The Chieftain of Skull Island aka Kundu Hite, he also served as caretaker. He hopped on board and we were on our way to his ancient burial grounds.

After a short ride, the assistant head man jumped out of the small motorized boat, and pulled it ashore. We followed his lead. On shore we felt a ghostly presence. We scrambled behind Chief Eddie, tripping over the black lava rock in our sandals, until we reached a clearing. A hut brimming with human skulls sat ominously on top of a black lava platform. Hundreds more littered the landscape.

Silence shrouded the island. Chief Eddie spoke, "These are my ancestors."

His aide pulled out a large triton shell. With a powerful breath he blew into a carved hole; until a loud, deep sound resonated from it. "That is how we call our people," he said.

Russ and I watched and listened with reverent curiosity. Chief Eddie explained how the Rovaina warriors of Kunda Hite rowed their war canoes to far away islands to go on head hunting raids. "This went on for hundreds of years," he said.

We'd been told the practice had only recently come to an end.

Bad karma supposedly resulted from picking up a skull or being photographed with one. Who were we to question the wisdom of the ancients? We stuck our hands in our pockets and returned to the boat, possibly two of the few ever to have escaped Skull Island.

Enough of the fascinating local culture and antiquity, the time had arrived to go diving. This activity in the Solomon Islands reflected World War II history. The archipelagos served as the site of a major campaign in the Pacific. The Japanese occupied the area, using large freighters to bring in supplies. The Allies fought back. *Toa Maru*, a transport ship damaged by the United States, ran aground and sunk off Gizo in 1943.

Over time *Toa Maru* evolved into a fantastic dive site, rife with life. A coral garden developed and flourished in the warm ocean. Saki bottles, tanks, supplies, a motorcycle and war-related debris strewn about the shipwreck, made for intriguing viewing. Sea turtles and mantra rays glided through the portals. A profusion of colorful fish flitted about the coral heads.

One pesky clownfish, Chuckles, I will never forget. That bright orange frisky fellow, with three white stripes, measured in at two inches, each feisty.

Clownfish and anemones live in a symbiotic relationship. Perhaps I swam by too close to his home; Chuckles began attacking my face mask. I'd swim away; he followed me and continued pecking at my mask. My eyes crossed as I looked at him. The assault lasted for several minutes. I wasted a lot of air laughing. It's highly entertaining being attacked by a clownfish.

Distraction free, I continued exploring the *Toa Maru*. One end of the ship lies on its side at forty-feet, the other end at one-hundred-thirty-feet. Staying on the shallow end allowed me plenty of time to explore before surfacing. Viewing the *Toa Maru* provided a glimpse of history frozen in time. I could almost picture Japanese soldiers ambling around the deck.

The next dive site, Grand Central Station, abounded in sea life, beautifully framed with hard and soft corals. The dive master informed us there were over two-hundred-seventy different species of fish. "Second highest fish count in the world," he said. I believe it. It seemed as if we were in an aquarium filled by Noah for the ark. We observed an astounding array of many different species. Sharks, lionfish, and barracuda linger as the most memorable.

The diving exceeded our expectations, but the memories we made were far from complete. A unique feature of the Solomon Islands was the chance to experience what others had before us. Plum Pudding Island aka Kennedy Island offered one of these opportunities.

John F. Kennedy commanded the *PT109*, when it received damage rammed by a Japanese destroyer during WWII. His ship sunk; Kennedy swam to shore.

The Gizo Hotel offered day trips to the island. "Let's go. Sounds exciting," I said. We were whisked to Kennedy Island—castaways for a day.

Dolphins cavorted offshore as we suited up to go snorkeling. The aquatic endeavor proved outstanding. Current flowed freely on the back side of the island. The depth exceeded that necessary for a dive. A variety of trees provided shade and a cool breeze buffered the tropical heat.

I'm certain we didn't replicate Kennedy's shipwreck experience. He probably didn't have snorkeling gear and ham sandwiches, but it stirred deep emotions to imagine his plight.

Time on the island passed quickly; shadows began to fall. The dim whir of a boat motor in the distance became audible. Our Plum Pudding maroon drew to a close. Unlike Kennedy, we'd planned our arrival and departure.

Russ and I left feeling melancholy. We both knew, we'd never return.

"Wonder if Kennedy shared the same sentiment?" I posed.

Sitting on the driftwood log, waiting for the boat to anchor, I pondered the phenomena of life. Others had come before us; others would come after. Our fate would be true only for us—no one else. I wonder what the future might hold.

Toa Maru clownfish, Chuckles protecting its anemone.
Solomon Islands

"Russ and Sue," après dive.
Solomon Islands

CHAPTER 16

Turks and Caicos—A Grand Time

Two pink flamingos, a salt shaker, lobster, conch and pelican stared at us from the pink stucco structure. A donkey grazing nearby looked up, hee-hawed showing his teeth, and then guffawed at the whimsical coat of arms. It decorated a government building on Grand Turk, a one-hour flight from Miami. "Beautiful by Nature" the Tourist Bureau declared. A look around seemed to confirm it.

Crystal-clear water gently lapped onto pink-tinged sand. A light wave washed ashore, causing the land and sea to intertwine in a frothy exchange.

Hints of fossil coral reef nuzzled the islet, giving the water a shade darker hue. Farther out, the sea continued the dramatic transition. The far, somber horizon meshed with the sapphire sky. Huge, billowing clouds with silver underpinnings floated above, creating yet another subtle layer of pigmentation.

Nature painted a masterpiece—the ideal seascape.

"Wow, it's beautiful here." My lofty thoughts plunged to terrestrial matters. "Wonder why the salt shaker is on that emblem?"

Russ didn't know, so he didn't respond. When he didn't know an answer, he pretended not to hear. "Why's that donkey standing in the middle of town?"

He again feigned hearing loss.

Neither of us knew. I'd discovered in our travels, much of the fun consisted of learning, problem-solving, and figuring things out

"Look at those. What the heck are they?" I wondered. Massive, round shallow ponds covered a considerable amount of space, just outside the center of town.

"Those are salt ponds." He knew that one. "They farmed salt on Grand Turk. Come to think of it, that's probably the reason for the salt shaker." He continued. He had a tendency to explain, beyond the extent my short attention span—about the length of a dehydrated inch-worm—could process.

"Channels to the ocean were dug on the low island. When complete, the farmers allowed the ponds to flood with sea water. The blocked inlets, after the liquid evaporated, left the salt behind. It would be raked, bagged and hauled off." He stopped for a moment, thought, then added, "May have been what the asses were for, to lug it around."

"That's interesting." I considered how telling this exchange with Russ proved. While he spent his brainpower to ascertain logical connections, my thoughts drifted to crafting a funny retort.

"So you're saying they hauled ass, er, um, I meant, the asses hauled?" *That's funny*, I thought. Good one. I pondered how my mind processed information. Cogitations flew around in my head like a hamster on an exercise wheel. A friend had once pointed out my brain worked like a comic strip. I thought, *Doesn't everyone's?* It took me awhile to figure out they didn't.

Russ' conjecture about the donkeys proved dead-on. The small pack animals were living remnants of the salt mining past. Their offspring wandered the island, such as the one standing in front of Victoria Public Library in downtown Grand Turk. Sort of cute to see them standing around, however their droppings mingled with the briny air to create a less than pleasant odor. The smell seemed counterintuitive to the beauty of the island.

"It's kind of stinky, let's go diving," I suggested. Arrangements were made to go out the next day.

The boat bounced over the choppy water. The majority of Grand Turk's dive sites lingered a short distance off the island's left side. The skipper dropped anchor at a spot called Rolling Hills, one of the farthest north destinations—not far from the lighthouse.

Our group dropped down a sheer vertical wall, descending into eighty-four degree water, to eighty-feet. Hard and soft corals blanketed the site with color. Orange encrusting sponges, at our maximum depth and below us, punctuated the drop-off. Healthy reef and a profusion of fish greeted us.

This dive, like others on Grand Turk teemed with sea life. When we finished diving the British West Indies, we'd be able to check off our fish list: angelfish, rock beauties, surgeonfish, graysbys, spadefish, trumpetfish, stingrays, gobies, butterfly, drums, grunts, and eels in addition to my favorites.

Among the various fish that populated the reefs, I fancied fairy basslets, among others. That's the name of a striking, bright orchid two-inch beauty that looked as though someone dipped the back half in a can of sunshine yellow paint.

Red hines, another favored species, had bug-eyes plastered on a light colored body, mottled with reddish-brown spots. *Mr. Magoo with the mumps*, I thought.

The pattern on a honeycomb boxfish, large octagonal cells in green, blue and yellow, might have been lifted from an aquacultured, genetically engineered food of the future. Its shape mimicked a three-quarters inflated balloon.

Camouflaged on the bottom dwelled the peacock flounder. Whitish-tan with a squashed-flat body, covered by blue, hollow markings, it looked like the unswept floor at a carnival ring toss. A fin stood oddly erect just behind its eye lumps.

The regal queen parrotfish could have passed for a National Geographic chart. Hues of blue and green blended together to create an oceanic map. The bright turquoise markings around its mouth looked like rivers emptying into the sea.

Nurse sharks, lobsters and turtles added to the underwater hodgepodge. Auxiliary members of the menagerie included crinoids, tubeworms, glass sponges and fan corals. The entire cast of the elaborate underwater production made for spectacular diving.

One day we were offered the opportunity to free dive for queen conch. "Sounds interesting. Could be fun. Let's do it." I loved trying out new activities.

Russ and I went to the docks, where we met the adventure craft. After a brief ride, the skipper bought the vessel to a halt, in about twenty feet of water. We jumped out, took a big breath of fresh air and swam to the bottom. Kicking down for the pink beauties that dwell on the seafloor wasn't only fun, but also fruitful.

After depositing our treasures into the watercraft, we climbed back aboard. Gear stowed; the captain steered the boat toward a sandy atoll.

"Grab the helm. I'm going to drop anchor," the skipper said. A crewman eased the shallow draft boat close to the deserted shore.

Russ, I and the other conch-divers hopped off, a mollusk in each hand. With a splash, we landed in about two-to-three-feet of calm water. Each of us waded toward the beach to clean our marine mollusks.

Almost immediately, a group of southern stingrays appeared. "We feed them," the deck hand said as he held out a handful of conch. They must have known lunchtime had arrived. They came right up. I balked.

"I've never seen a stingray near the beach," I said. We later learned they have a wide range of habitat from one-foot to eighty-feet.

"Don't be afraid. They won't hurt you," the skipper's assistant said.

Well, wouldn't be the dumbest thing I've ever done, I'm going to pet it.

Several more appeared and rubbed up against my leg, knocking me off balance, before I had the chance to.

Russ and I joined in hand-feeding the stingrays. Because their eyes were on the top, and their mouths were on the bottom, they couldn't see what they ate. We held the food out, so they could take it from our hands. As they fed, I considered how strange they looked.

Stingrays resembled burned, triangular-shaped pancakes. A darkish-brown top covered a white underside. Most of the gliding crepes looked about three to four feet across, but a couple of whoppers may have exceeded five feet.

In their creation, it appeared as though the batter dribbled and left a trail of dough behind, creating a long tail that resembled a whip. Two venomous barbs extended from the base of the tail and angled toward the back. Eyes bubbled up like air pockets above their bodies.

The aquatic flapjacks swam by flapping their vertices up and down. As awkward as they sound described, they moved with a beautiful, graceful, elegance—nothing short of a well orchestrated ballet.

"This is weird, but amazing." I commented. "I've seen stingrays fly off the bottom, if they're lying hidden in the sand, and you accidentally kick them with a fin—but, I've never seen them like this."

Upon depletion of the handouts, they disappeared.

"Who wants to crack the conch?" the gregarious islander asked. A huge smile swept over his face, as if he may know something we didn't know.

"I will." I volunteered for things unknown. No thought, no second-guessing, no consideration of consequences, that's me. *How hard can it be?* I thought.

The, I-know-something-you-may-not-know fellow proceeded to demonstrate how easy it was using a hatchet. He quickly extradited the meat from the shell, then handed me the tool.

I gave it a fast whack. Nothing. Tried again. Same result. Made several more attempts with no effect. I placed the conch on the beach and frantically pounded on it. "Okay, I give up. What's the trick?"

After he wiped the tears from his eyes, and regained his composure, the jokester said, "You have to..." he started laughing again. "You have to break the shell near the apex to release the vacuum, and then you can pull the foot out." *That's pretty good*, I thought. *He pulled my leg by not telling me to pull the foot.*

"Oh." I had no future comment. I enjoyed listening to everyone's laughter.

Conch diving proved entertaining, however we'd been so impressed with B.W.I.'s underworld world, we wanted to do more diving. Russ arranged to dive: the Canyon, McDonald's and the Library. The last two sites in particular had us madly checking off our fish list.

"Did you get the blue tang?"

"That wasn't a blue tang, it was a doctorfish."

"I really think it was blue tang." We knew just enough about fish to get confused. Many of the darn things looked alike.

"Well, we can't check it off unless we're sure which one it was."

"I got a better idea. We'll check off both, that way we'll be sure we got the right one."

At times our approaches differed. He had the list and the pen. Neither got checked off.

Tunnel, our last dive on Grand Turk, proved our favorite. It lay at the far end of the island from Rolling Hills. An interesting site, the wall filled with tunnels and cuts, offered lots of diverting places to explore and swim through.

We made several dives off Providenciales (Provo) Island, Turks and Caicos. Russ and I dove the northwest point, the Crack and Shark Hotel.

Diving proved pleasant, however not as spectacular as Grand Turk. The boat ride at forty-minutes also took longer. A streamlined man-eater gliding close by created the most memorable Provo moment; along with Fifi, the French dive master, who broke out bottles of wine on the return trip.

At sixty-feet, in open water, Russ heard Fifi banging on his tank. My buddy looked up to see the frightening predator a mere five-feet away. "I looked at him," Russ said, "and he turned and swam away." Russ got a great shot of an eight-foot Caribbean reef shark.

On West Caicos, our final dive destination, we stopped at Highway to Heaven and Melissa Cove. Again sharks appeared to be the main attraction. The dive operation impressed us, but stinky, little Grand Turk still offered the best diving.

We happily wrapped up our diving, and I unhappily put our Personal Record of Fish Sightings away. "I really think we could have checked off another couple of fish." I never had an obsession prior to the idiot fish list. "Well, maybe next time." I reluctantly stowed it in the suitcase.

"I read there's a conch farm on the island. Suppose to be the only one in the world. Let's go find it," I said. Off we went to see the overgrown snails.

The facility looked abandoned. I suppose there isn't a lot to do when you're waiting for a conch to grow at a snail's pace. A dozen or more, round shallow concrete holding tanks, thirty-to-forty-feet in diameter dominated a large area. Small conch littered the bottom—hundreds occupied each tank. Next to the ponds, lay tall stacks of empty Purina Conch Chow bags.

"You're kidding. Purina Conch Chow? That sounds a little fishy to me," I said. "That reminds me, I miss Fuzzy and Woolley."

"We'll be going home tomorrow. We could take them some." Our kitties, like us, loved to eat.

"I bet they'd like it." While ruminating on his idea, I came to a conclusion. "Life is like a banquet. Our adventures are like dessert." I relished the thought, the most philosophical I'd ever had. I couldn't wait to have another helping.

Wild donkey standing in front of Victoria Public Library.
Cockburn Town, Grand Turk, Turks & Caicos

Coat of Arms, Government Building.
Cockburn Town, Grand Turk, Turks & Caicos

CHAPTER 17

"Falling" in Love with the San Juans

The rounded stones lay on the beach like tiddlywinks spilled on a mat. Slick, golden brown ribbons of bull kelp with bulbous heads, threaded over the pebbles. Driftwood, like phantom figures raised from the grave, lay strewn helter-skelter on the sand.

The islands jutted out of the cerulean water. Like lily pads in a pond, they populated the Salish Sea in America's northwest corner. Gentle, verdant slopes introduced Mt. Baker and Mt. Rainer, the jagged, snow-covered peaks that rose in sharp contrast behind them.

Our penchant for scuba diving, not only gave us an excuse to visit tropical and exotic destinations, but also quaint and charming places here at home. The San Juan Archipelago—touted as "Real Islands. Real Close," by the visitor' bureau became a favored destination. It proved unnecessary to leave the country to find exceptional diving; the water just wasn't nearly as warm.

Washington State Ferries serve Orcas, San Juan, Shaw and Lopez Islands. The leviathans caromed from one island to the next, like objects in a pinball machine. Private boat or small plane provides access to others, including Sucia, Patos, and Waldron Islands.

Each port of call entices with its own distinct personality. Orcas' ambience is laid-back, an artsy destination suited to gallery hopping. San Juan is home to humming, lively Friday Harbor, the boating hub of the group. Lopez's flat terrain and bucolic scenery allures bicyclists. Shaw, the quiet pip-squeak of the bunch, has a few parks—but lacks tourist facilities.

Orcas Island in autumn displays a special magic. It won our hearts. A stroll down Enchanted Forest Lane beckoned from the first footstep ashore. Peaceful solitude prevailed. A maple leaf twirled to the ground like a ballerina performing a pirouette.

The countryside burned with brilliant red and bright gold deciduous trees. Annuals nestled in forests of pine, cedar and fir. Deep purple berries and waxy yellow apples hung long forgotten on derelict plants. The scent of the fruit and trees commingled to create an autumnal potpourri.

Nature provided gentle reminders that summer waned. A slight hint of a chill punctuated the air. A squirrel scurried by with an acorn.

"Today's a beautiful day, but the critter knows winter's on the way. Stashing away those provisions," I noted, as we watched the hoarder stockpile his treasure.

A variety of artistic and creative endeavors flourished on Orcas. Residents knitted sweaters, threw pottery, blew glass, designed jewelry and painted pictures. The island served as a source of never-ending inspiration.

An artist's studio sat beside the gravel road. Peacocks, trailing their long plumage, strutted by a rustic, brick kiln. Native plants grew helter-skelter around the dwelling. Multiple cuttings of plants waiting to go into the ground, loafed in a variety of colorful, earthenware pots. The dwelling didn't appear unkempt, but rather gave the impression of simply too much to do.

In a ramshackle outbuilding that sat perpendicular to the house, tack hung on rusty nails. A potter's wheel sat in the center, encrusted with clay. Surrounding it, as if distributed by a Spirograph, more light-colored, dried mud lay splattered on the concrete floor.

An amiable, plump, rosy-cheeked, red-haired woman appeared from the house. “Greetings, and how are yah both this fine day?” She spoke with a slight brogue. “Would yah like to come in and see my work?” She walked with a slight limp as she led us into her humble bungalow. The aroma of freshly-baked blueberry muffins wafted from the kitchen.

She proceeded to show us her hand-thrown ceramics; pots, tea sets, plates, mugs, vases and an olio of other creations.

As she held up one of her designs, I noticed a thirty-pound, orange tabby with white paws and tummy. The fluffy lion leaned up against a wall, then slid down it. “Main Coon—they’re a large breed.” She hurried over to give him a hug. “Ah me puss, Punkin’, don’t cha worry, Mom loves yah,” she reassured the cat.

After a too short visit to Orcas, my buddy and I caught the ferry to San Juan. On this passage the water imitated an ice rink—not always the case.

Sunshine reigned as the ferryboat cruised toward Friday Harbor. As it neared the dock, a gentle ripple folded and distorted the reflection of the evergreen trees.

Their sloping home leaned down to greet arriving passengers.

Sailboats floated lazily by, wiling away time, as if they knew possibly no better pastime existed.

Friday Harbor buzzed with activity. The harbormaster, located in a white, gazebo-type building, directed heavy traffic around the docks as the transport unloaded. Fisherman, sailors and mariners wielded powerboats, sailboats and yachts; they sought a slip for the night. Old salts and sea dogs competed for a place just to tie up for awhile.

While ambling into town, an ice cream shop reached out and grabbed us—like a hook at a Vaudeville theater. Russ and I succumbed, and selected our favorites.

“I’ll have two scoops; one vanilla, one chocolate. In a dish,” Russ stated with authority.

After considerable thought and reconsideration, I guessed, I'd like, "A double chocolate chunk and a strawberry cheesecake in a waffle cone, no maybe…"

Our selections reflected our personalities. Russ made ultra-conservative choices. He knew what he wanted. I, an extreme risk taker, never quite sure, just rolled the dice. After I did, I often didn't know whether I liked where they landed.

He: a yin, taciturn, super-smart, Pisces, pessimistic, first-born, perfectionist. Me: a yang, talkative, slightly-above average intelligence (because I wrote this), Aries, optimistic, easy-going, middle child. He loved peace and quiet. I loved noise and confusion.

My basic desire, to have fun, differed from his basic desire, to have control. At times we didn't see eye-to-eye, unremarkable because he hit the yardstick at nearly six feet. I barely made it past five. If not from different planets, we were at least two dissimilar species.

"How did you two *ever* meet?" a friend had once asked me.

"We met at work," I'd replied, realizing it sounded like a cliché. "Otherwise I don't think our paths would have ever crossed." Employed by an electronics firm, I pushed papers around in an ill-fitting job. Russ installed two-way radios. If we'd landed in occupations that reflected our real selves, I'd probably have been a trapeze artist flying through the air for Cirque du Soleil; Russ a rocket scientist inventing new methods of space travel for NASA.

Differing delights in hand, we climbed the steep hillside into the historic old town. Wood buildings from the turn of the century, like elderly statesman, rose proud on both sides of the street. A classic brick bank, an arcade-type edifice, and country saloon facade created an Old West ambience. I could almost visualize the sheriff and his posse chasing an outlaw down 1st Street.

A dozen aged structures housed fine dining restaurants. Other timeworn construction provided a dwelling for galleries and shops. A barber pole, resembling a giant peppermint stick, executed a slow twirl in front of one of the centenarian storefronts.

The uphill trek led to the San Juan Historical Museum. I perused the posted information. "Pig War? The Americans and British fought a war over a pig?" Incredulous would have been an understatement for my reaction.

"Yes," the retired, white-haired volunteer serving as curator replied. "In 1859 the United States and Britain jointly occupied the island. An on-going dispute developed regarding the water boundary. The San Juans lay between Vancouver Island and the North American mainland. It remained unsettled, so the Americans occupied one side and the British the other."

"What's that got to do with the pig?" I asked.

"Well, everything was going fine," she said, then breathed out heavily and brushed some fine, snowy hair away from her face. "Then, an American farmer shot a pig that rooted in his potato patch. It belonged to the Hudson's Bay Company. The pig—the only casualty—triggered the war. You can visit both outposts, if you have a way to get there," she added.

"Wow, that's wild. I noticed a wheels-for-hire on the way here. Let's go back, borrow a couple of scooters, and check it out," I said.

My buddy and I returned to the vehicle lending lot. Rental required the completion of a moped safety class, demonstrating our skills on the roadway. During the exam I got lost—so it took a little longer than normal. I found my way back and somehow passed. Fortunately, navigation skills weren't a requisite. With helmets on head, and map in hand, we were on our way.

"These things sure don't go fast. Good thing it's not far. We'll have to go to both ends of the island." I shouted, so Russ could hear me over the road noise.

We passed by a century-old, white church adorned by a tall steeple. Beside it, in a pasture, placid cattle lounged—some grazed, a few reposed. From a distance, they looked like a Whitman's Sampler spilled out on the green grass: butter cream, caramel, milk chocolate and dark fudge.

Russ and I stopped to look at the map. "Beautiful country. Did you see that herd back there? Holy cow, they appeared so pastoral," I joked.

The San Juan National Historical Park, English Camp, the sign read. A Union Jack flapped in front of a squat, viewing tower that shed white paint. It abutted a rocky beach that formed a perfect, horseshoe-shaped bay.

A round, formal garden with geometric inner patterns in seamless symmetry, seemed to announce the properness of the encampment. As though to further emphasize the civility, a white picket fence surrounded the circular landscaping.

"Royal Marines imported their culture," the informational tour guide said. "They held social events including galas, teas and balls."

"Guess they enjoyed the good life here on this beautiful inlet, surrounded by woodland. Not bad. Let's go see how the Americans fared," I said.

As I mounted my moped, I caught a glimpse of something overhead. "Wow, look at that," I said pointing toward the sky. "Awesome." A huge eagle soared above. His wingspan must have exceeded six feet. His dark brown body, white head and tail, created an impressive sight against the flawless azure sky. He disappeared into the adjacent towering evergreens.

"Remember what the curator told us? The largest concentration of bald eagles in the continental United States is located here."

"Yeah, but this is the English Camp. Bald eagles are a symbol of America. They should be on the other side of the island."

"I'm shocked. I can't believe it," I said as I stood staring at the American Camp. "This can't be the same island. It's so arid and desolate." An enormous barren prairie with little more than two dilapidated buildings and a gun emplacement stared back.

In stark contrast to British Camp's lush forest and tree-sheltered bay; the over-grazed, windswept, headquarters of the American Army looked pathetic.

On the National Park tour, the guide had told us that while the English delighted in the finer things and elaborate celebrations, the Americans drank and got depressed. Due to their desolation, some even committed suicide.

"Guess we got the short end of the stick," I commented.

"For awhile, but in the end, we won. It's not like they didn't accomplish anything. The park's spokesperson mentioned the author of *Robert's Rules of Order* served here."

"That's right." The military officer got transferred often. At one place, he had been asked to preside over a church meeting. It ended up in a donnybrook.

"Parliamentary anarchy befell the gathering," he'd said. "So, he wrote the book to bring order to the chaos."

"Guess I learned something," I said.

"What's that?"

"If you've got too much time on your hands, write a book." The San Juans had once again proved a source of inspiration.

Although ferrying to the islands provided an enjoyable transport; the novelty wore off, and drawbacks existed. Schedules limited travel times. The queues, especially during peak travel season, could stretch into four hour waits. Our destination remained limited to four selections.

In a worst-case-scenario, if there wasn't space available, or we missed the last ferry, we couldn't get to work on Monday. This crimped our freewheeling style, and it got expensive. The fare, determined by length, continued to increase. Our truck, pulling our 18-foot tri-hull, outboard on a 25-foot trailer, measured 50-feet in length.

To overcome the inconveniences and expense, Russ devised a solution.

He traded *Ah Baloney*, our old boat, for a lovingly worn, but adequate, 27-foot sleep-aboard Carver. Once we had *Escape*, we were free to do so.

Our new, aged yacht got hauled up I-5 North to Anacortes, and launched often, from late spring to late fall. My buddy and I could leave after work on Friday and get there late, but exhausted, that evening.

Our alternate transportation opened up a whole new world. Limited access Washington State Parks in the San Juans now fell within the realm of possibility. Not only did this greatly improve our ability to move about the islands, we could come and go as we pleased.

I became astounded by how much more the archipelagos had to offer. Sucia Island and Jones Island especially delighted me. Wildlife abounded and thrived on the undisturbed, natural settings.

On Sucia, Russ usually docked at Fossil Bay. The translucent, emerald green water wooed us. Five more anchorages existed on the island, all accessible by the hiking trails. No vehicular traffic or roads existed on the water surrounded parks.

My buddy and I would awaken to cry of seabirds and water lapping against the side of the boat.

I'd stretch and yawn, then put the coffee on. It simmered in the dented, tin percolator that sat atop the alcohol stove. After savoring a cup of joe on the dock's picnic tables, we'd don our boots and hit the trail.

Our favorite hike culminated at a promontory with an expansive view. After finding a place to plop, we'd watch the boats float by. Spinner dolphins, in pairs, might leap out of the water. The Orca pod could make an appearance. Bald eagles or ospreys at times soared overhead. Deer frequently grazed openly.

"This is a beautiful world we live in," I commented to Russ as we lazed on the rock, looking out on the Salish Sea. "I think I could be a seal. It wouldn't be a bad life." As much as I loved it there, I knew we needed to get going.

I reluctantly rose, taking a mental snapshot hoping to commit it to memory. Russ and I returned to the dusty trail. I shuffled through the fallen leaves, as we sauntered back through the peeling, red-barked manzanitas and evergreens.

The fresh water station grabbed my attention. "Hurry up. Don't want to miss the current," Russ said, as I took a long swig.

"You're right about that." Diving at the wrong time could lead to problems. The tide and currents could change dramatically without any warning.

Russ eased the boat away from the dock on a perfect San Juan day. Air temperature lingered around seventy degrees. Water temperature would be a not-quite-so-pleasant, forty-something degrees. I chuckled as I recalled chatting with a tourist from the Sunshine State. "We dive in Florida, but it never would have occurred to me to dive here," she had said.

Russ reached our intended dive spot and anchored. He dropped the dingy, *Dinky* off the back of the transom, then played out fifty-feet of line to grab upon return.

The cold temperature mandated wearing a dry suit—an air-insulated, waterproof garment—for comfort, although it still felt bone-chilling. The buoyancy of garb necessitated a back-breaking, forty-pounds of lead to sink. The onerous weight belt and cumbersome ankle weights prevented surfacing feet first.

I mused about diving the frigid Campbell River in Canada. I'd just purchased my dry suit, after wearing a wet suit for years. I soon discovered that dry suit diving demanded far more technical expertise.

I delighted in the fact, that if I pushed the magic button on the upper portion of the suit, air from the tank filled the baggy rubber covering, chasing the chill. The more I depressed it, the happier I felt. As the dive went on, the prolonged exposure made me colder. I jabbed it some more.

After one last punch, I noted a strange sensation. I felt my feet slowly starting to rise. The action intensified. I went topsy-turvy as my feet zoom past my head. The next thing I knew, I landed on the surface, fully inflated, resembling the Michelin tire man.

Talk about bursting out at seams! The air had expanded as I ascended, making it even more balloon-like. Luckily, it wasn't a deep dive. I could have been in real trouble. Sheer luck saved me once again.

My thoughts returned to the task at hand. After "spitting" our masks—to avoid having them fog up—and pulling on our fins, we rolled off the back of *Escape*.

"Yowza! I can never get used to how cold this water is." It slapped me in the face sending a shock wave through my body. Russ didn't reply, as usual. He just raised his BC hose over his head to descend. We floated down into the numbing, silty, forest green sea.

At maximum, the visibility may have been forty-feet. Russ had shot an azimuth before we descended. The murkiness demanded excellence at underwater navigation. Diving these waters, made me appreciate the importance of compass skills. We'd practiced them prior to scuba certification, by walking around with brown, paper bags over our heads.

My buddy and I followed a wall down, keeping an eye on our gauges—which were superseded by dive computers. A miscalculation could put us in open water at one-hundred-feet, someplace we didn't want to be. At fifty-feet we hit a thermocline—the water got even colder. I wonder how that could be possible.

At sixty-feet, we attained neutral buoyancy, and began our dive.

Satisfied with our bearings, Russ and I began looking around. Dozens of pectens burst up from the bottom in a flurry. Their pink shells, with stem-like blue eyes and white cilia waving in the current, swam by resembling clicking castanets.

Pectens, commonly known as scallops, are good eating. Russ scooped up a few—previous to regulations later enacted, into the goody bag for dinner.

When we first began diving, pinto abalone up to eight-inches had a legal limit, but they have long since been closed. We'd take a few back to the camper, slice them thin, then sauté them in garlic and butter. Chewy strips, but delicious. The iridescent shells with mother-of-pearl inner layers dazzled.

Rock scallops, another delight from the depths, incited drool. The shells, as large as dinner plates, adhered to the rock with the equivalent of extra-strength superglue. Divers used knives to pry them out, leaving the lower shells behind.

The meat of one scallop could measure three inches across. Similar to the abalone, though not as tough, they were tender and tasty

Two eyes peeked out from a crevice. A curious wolf eel wondered who might be visiting. He poked his head out. The giant-jowled oddity looked like a macabre Richard Nixon with uncontrolled impetigo.

"Did you see that wooffle?" I thought our dive instructor had asked, after we'd surfaced from a dive. A high-energy person, he spoke like he moved, rapidly. For a long time after that I thought a wooffle might be similar to a Star Trek tribble. I visualized it as a sea creature resembling a sea urchin, but perhaps less prickly.

"A wolf *eel*?" I couldn't believe it when Russ decided to let me in on the joke. "I wondered why you guys all snickered whenever I mentioned one."

I spotted what I thought to be a log—but it moved. As it swam away, I realized it was a ling cod. Females during spawning season could become aggressive. White masses, the eggs, stuck to rocks meant beware. The fish had been rumored to attack divers to protect their offspring.

A number of Northwest divers relish spear fishing for ling cod—one big, ugly, prehistoric-looking fish—but delicious. The delicacy looked like something put through the wringer, and reassembled wrong. The lips appeared to have been reattached in error, they were too large. A small ling measures three-feet; a big ling has to be carted off the dock in a wheelbarrow.

Continuing to peruse the bottom, we spotted an octopus' hole. The lairs were easily identified by the copious stack of fish bones and shells near the entrance. "That octopus' hangout looked like an ogre's den," Russ had once commented.

The shy cephalopods didn't make an appearance on this dive, but we'd witnessed an eight-foot, reddish-brown Giant Pacific Octopus change color and texture to match surrounding rocks.

Visibility improved as we ascended along the wall into shallower water. At twenty-five-feet, we encountered a kelp forest. The brownish-yellow flexible stem, firmly rooted to the bottom, swayed to and fro in the current. Narrow blades, resembling cheerleader's pom-poms, extended from the bulbous float that lay near the surface. Seaweed entanglement could cause problems. Russ kept a knife strapped to his lower leg, in case we needed to cut the vegetation away.

Russ checked his gauge. He ran low on air; he used more than I did. Also, the slack tide waned. A ten-foot or more variation occurred with the changing tide. The current could rip through at five mph or greater. We'd observed boaters caught off-guard by sudden encounters with previously hidden, emerging rocks.

At ten-feet we made a safety stop, and then surfaced. I grabbed *Dinky*'s rope, pulled myself back to the boat, and climbed aboard. Russ followed. "Nice dive," I mumbled. I didn't enunciate well, my lips remained numb from the cold.

My favorite time had arrived, après dive—a hot shower, followed by a bask in the sun—simple, pure joy.

By the time we'd doffed our dry suits, enjoyed our shower and warmed up; the tide had begun to churn. I pulled anchor, Russ took the helm. He started off slow, accelerated, trimmed out *Escape*, and then put it on a plane. *Escape* flew across the water trailing a white, frothy rooster tail.

"The sea is getting restless," Russ said. He re-trimmed to accommodate the change. The conditions which could change rapidly, did. Soon Russ and I found ourselves, in our 27-foot boat, trapped in thirty-foot seas. Waves didn't just break over the bow, they broke over the cabin.

I went down to hide in the living quarters, while Russ struggled to keep the bow of the boat into the gale. I watched the water engulf the windshield, seeming to swallow the vessel. Meanwhile Russ man-handled *Escape*, if it got sideways, we could roll.

Sets of waves arrived close together, making it impossible to see the next group. Tossed on top of a wave, we could see around us; but when pitched down in the troth, we could see nothing.

The intensity of the experience made it seem like it lasted an eternity, but in reality it occurred during a half-hour period. As quickly as the seas had boiled, they returned to a simmer. A great sense of relief sweep over us. "Were you afraid we were going to roll?" bug-eyed, I asked Russ, after the seas subsided.

"No, buddy, I was driving." Love that confidence, that's quintessential Russ.

Sucia would be the evening's destination; we headed in that direction.

After situating, we took *Dinky* to set the crab trap. I rowed out a short distance—several times because I had a tendency to travel in a circular motion.

Russ opened a can of cat food with a v-shaped opener. The tin got tossed into the trap, along with a lead weight to sink it. Over the side it went. It hit the water with a splash, and then sunk into the shallow bay.

I circumnavigated us back for dinner—fresh seafood dockside.

At sunset the group campsite beckoned. Weary picnic tables sat scattered around a grand, ash-filled pit. Makeshift kindling, driftwood, sat stacked near by.

My buddy and I found a place to roost with a view of the fire and water.

Swapping stories, sharing wine and laughs, toasting marshmallows by the fire, we enjoyed our like-minded onshore companions.

The next morning, time arrived to check the crab pot. Russ pulled it in hand-over-hand. The resistance often gave a clue to how many crabs might be inside. "Seems too easy," Russ said. Not a good sign. Zilch. At times it crawled with sweet, tasty rock crab—but not this time.

"Darn, looks like we got skunked." Much of the fun of crabbing lay in not knowing the outcome. Although, crab for dinner would have been nice.

Upon return, I spooled up our coiled mooring line and put the bumpers in. Russ eased *Escape* toward an adjacent shore.

Patos Island housed a retired Coast Guard station and lighthouse. Abandoned buildings sat overlooking the sea, adjacent to the beacon tower, which rested further out on the point.

Previous to automation, it appeared the structures served as military housing. Russ and I peeked in one of units. It looked like someone had just stepped out for milk. Appliances remained in the kitchen. Signs of life—magazines, mattresses, cooking utensils—lay strewn about. The forgotten quarters had a sort of eerie, post-apocalyptic feel. "This is kind of creepy," I said.

"If we get going now, we should be able to make it home before too late tonight."

Using the onboard compass, Russ guided us back toward Anacortes.

Sailing across the channel could be tricky. I recalled a previous trip. One morning, on the way out, we encountered fog—thick as condensed-cream-of-mushroom soup. Russ and I couldn't see our feet. Ghost ships appeared out of the mist.

A barge and tug tow line could be deadly, as could colliding with another boat, or being run over by a ferry. We stayed out of the shipping channel and listened for the warning blasts from the ferry boats, which were guided by radar.

Russ found a small inlet along shore to hug. We waited. Four hours later, when the air warmed, the fog cleared.

"Well, another great trip to the San Juans," I said, as we loaded *Escape* back onto the trailer.

"It's always interesting coming up here. We never know what we're going to find."

"I do."

"Okay. What's that?"

"A good time."

Multi-mast sailing ship afloat in the Salish Sea (designated as the official inland marine waters of Washington State and British Columbia in 2010). San Juan Islands, Washington

CHAPTER 18

Dominica—Pure Energy But No Lights

The ancient fort towered above the harbor; parts of its walls still encased the old city. Old San Juan's Spanish heritage created a portal into history. Sixteenth-century buildings and hundred-year-old houses intermingled with sidewalk cafes and tourist shops. Shaded benches and bronze statues loitered in the town square.

Ponce de Leon, seeker of the Fountain of Youth, arrived in 1508. He stayed and established a settlement. Our visit would last only one day. Russ and I had stopped over en route to Dominica.

"I'd like to see the San Juan National Historic Site," I said. As we began trudging up the steep hill to the ancient strongholds, an open-air trolley passed.

"We could have taken it." Russ eyed the vehicle as it went by.

"Yeah, but this is great exercise. Maybe that's the secret of staying young."

Russ didn't care much for exertion. He huffed and puffed. We continued up.

Poking along gave us lots time to sightsee. Stucco *casas* with wrought-iron balconies lined the walkway. Pink and white bougainvillea cascaded from them.

Challenging hill—we used every excuse we could think of to stop and rest. "What beautiful trees. Do you know what they are?" I asked Russ.

"I'm not sure." He halted to take a prolonged look.

Eventually my buddy and I reached my destination.

El Morrow, a gigantic fortress built by the Spaniards, to keep marauders at bay loomed above us. I gazed out to sea. The expansive view from the rocky point proved impressive. I looked inward, toward the interior of the fort. Extensive grounds littered with turrets, cannons, barracks and other artifacts of its colonial past defined the bastion. "Glad we came up. Well worth the effort, huh?"

Silence.

After exploring the engrossing historical site, Russ and I went back down the hill, much faster than we had gone up.

Super-class cruise ships crowded the marina. San Juan served as the port-of-origin for many of the luxury liners that sailed the Caribbean. Due to the influx of passengers, numerous tourist facilities existed. We sought a place for dinner.

It didn't take long to find a café. By candlelight my buddy and I enjoyed a mouthwatering meal of grilled red snapper—swimming in garlic sauce, and fried plantains. A wandering *trovador*, replete with black *sombrero*, strummed Spanish love songs on his acoustic guitar.

I scheduled a Bacardi Rum factory tour and then drifted off into a deep, dreamy sleep.

Oops, overslept. Free samples would have to wait. I threw everything back into our carry-on and we scurried off to the airport.

The flight plan took us over Montserrat. It had recently experienced a catastrophic eruption. The massive ash flow down one side, from the explosion, remained visible from the air. The sullen, gray impacted area lingered.

In contrast, Dominica—the Caribbean's Nature Island, blew me away. Flying in, as we circled and began our descent, it seemed as though the plane were being sucked into a kaleidoscopic vortex.

A cloud-like aura, dissected by a vivid rainbow, seemed to enshroud the island. The high mountains, in the heart of the rugged interior, loomed like jade-green sentinels. They guarded the valleys and shores, the waterfalls and rivers.

I watched the landscape grow closer; the landing gear dropped. The wheels hit the ground. "I can't wait to go exploring."

Russ leaned over to take a gander. "It looks like we picked a good one."

On the long ride from the airport to our hotel, the taxi driver gave us the grand tour. He followed a narrow, winding road for miles through tropical rain forest.

Dense vegetation, punctuated by tropical flowers, spilled onto the lane's shoulder. The air, scented by lemongrass and wild orchids, wafted in our open windows.

A medley of unfamiliar birds greeted us as we registered at the hotel's outdoor lobby. "You're welcome to attend the beach barbeque on Sunday," our host said.

"I'm sure glad we came," I said. Robust men pounded out reggae on steel drums. Guests chatted and moved to the rhythmic music. Rum punch flowed freely; fried chicken served generously. The afternoon BBQ went on well into the night. It seemed locals loved to party—so we did.

Late the following morning, my buddy and I went diving. We experienced a first, a female dive master. Although I'd found a few kindred spirits who enjoyed diving, they'd all been males. She proved quite capable of piloting the large aluminum boat and could even back it up without hitting anything.

Yet another unprecedented event occurred—I spied a seahorse. I'd observed countless critters while diving, but the seahorse galloped off with my "Cutest Little Thing" title. I had friends that dove for years, and never glimpsed a seahorse. They harbored camouflaging qualities that made them difficult to spot, perhaps that explains why.

I swam at a shallow depth, close to shore, when I noticed it. The spiny, brown, two-inch fish had wrapped its curly tail around a bright orange branching sponge. Swaying to and fro in the current, its long snout and bug eyes made it look like a tipsy cartoon character.

As I watched the animated curlicue fish, another one came galloping along.

The anchored mini-pony let go, changed color, and linked tails with the new arrival. They engaged in a dance, spinning and twirling around, performing a delightful display. After awhile they separated and trotted away.

My awe only began with the miniature marine cuties. The vibrant multicolored reef that lay below the surface dazzled. Rumored to be Jimmy Buffet's favorite place to dive, after a few, I understood why.

Russ and I tallied eight dives during our visit. Some we enjoyed so much, we did twice. We dove near Portsmouth, St. Joseph, and Scott's Head—all boat dives a short distance offshore.

A variety of colorful sponges: branching, glass, stove pipe, azure and pink vase blended together to create an Impressionistic masterwork. I'd needed a mask with corrective lenses for awhile. Giant anemones, which blanketed the site, proved just as stunning.

Tubeworms, in nearly every color of the visible spectrum, undulated in slow motion. Soft corals and brain corals added pizzazz. Moray eels, green and brown-spotted, played peek-a-boo out of nooks and crannies, adding a bit of fun.

Mollusks added brilliance. Bright orange clams and shiny pink conchs decorated the bottom, like ornaments the cat knocked off the Christmas tree.

A teeny long-legged spider crab rested on sapphire blue encrusting sponge. An itty-bitty coral banded shrimp lounged on a rock. Other crustaceans—lobsters and crabs, peered out of hidden places adding a splash of mystery.

If this all sounds amazing, it was. Furthermore after diving for awhile, I realized that for everything I saw—there was probably far more I hadn't. The diving we deemed awesome. Dominica won our "Favorite-Place-to-Dive-Award: Caribbean," as Fiji had in the South Pacific.

The island offered outstanding diving, but we also wanted to do things we couldn't do elsewhere. A canoe trip up a jungle stream was one of those.

Frances, a tour guide, took our group up the Indian River. The waterway once provided a home to the Carib Indians. As he rowed upstream, he pointed out the jungle's inhabitants. "Look, a Jaco Parrot," he said. "We have over 150 different species of birds." Lizards, frogs, butterflies and snakes were also bought to our attention. "We'll be lucky if we see a boa constrictor," he added.

I figured we'd be lucky if we didn't, especially as we stopped to get out of the canoe. The heat and humidity made a bit of liquid refreshment seem like a fine idea. At the river's end lay Rahjah's Jungle Bar, a dirt floor covered by a tin roof.

Most group members enjoyed a Kubuli (local beer) at the wooden picnic table. As we sipped our brew, we watched a Rasta wove birds and fish from straws.

"This is for you, lovely lady," he said, as he handed me one of his completed works of art. He continued around the group, presenting one to each of the women in our party.

After expressing our gratitude—and checking for the reptilian hugger—each of us climbed into the canoe. Frances took us back down the river.

Dinner at an outdoor French Creole restaurant proved a real treat. I took a pass on mountain chicken (frog) and *agouti* (rodent) and went for the fresh catch.

The waiter served blue marlin steaks, family style, on a monstrous banana leaf that covered the length of the table. *What a great idea*, I thought, *no dishes*.

Having missed the Bacardi tour on San Juan, we were pleased to see that Dominica had its own facility, the Macoucherie Rum Factory.

Islanders used a water-driven mill to crush sugar cane. "It's one of the last in use in the Caribbean," the operator said. An inefficient system, the cane had to be run through the wringer multiple times, before all the liquid could be removed.

"That would drive me to drink the profits," I said quietly to Russ.

The liquid, once extracted, could be used to make sugar, molasses, or rum.

"Elixir of Bois Bande is special rum. It's made from Richeria Grandis tree bark," the factory worker told us.

Why does that sound familiar to me? I wondered. Then I remembered. Frances, our exuberant young guide, had pointed it out on the jungle trip. "From this tree," he'd said, "they make a very special drink. This is for the old guys, this is not for me." Everyone had laughed, except for the old guys.

Our island time languidly slipped away. One day remained. What a day it turned out to be.

Our final evening on the island coincided with the Grand Finale Beach Party for Dive Fest '99. I'd already determined the islanders liked to party, but this blow-out exceeded them all.

My buddy and I arrived via dive boat to Soufriere—population about 8,000—where the celebration took place. The craft provided safer transport than traveling the one lane road by car.

By the time we arrived, the village rocked. Mayhem might describe the scene.

"Wow, what a wild…" POOF. The fun came to an abrupt end, when the ear-splitting audio equipment blew a fuse. Almost every light in Soufriere went out. "Guess, the grand finale isn't going to have an encore," I said.

Passengers, who arrived by boat, took off their shoes and waded out to the waiting transport in total darkness. Each of us climbed back aboard.

The skippers swung the vessel around, pointing it up the coast.

Moonlight shone on the water. A balmy breeze blew through the open cabin. Russ and I sat snuggled up staring at the starry sky.

As we cruised back toward the hotel, I recalled an unusual hand painted sign. Nailed on a coconut tree at the party, scrawled on a weathered piece of wood—"It's nice to be nice." *What a lovely sentiment*, I thought.

I couldn't think of a nicer place to be, or a better place to dive.

Diving had given us excuses to visit some of the most heavenly places on the planet. We had more excuses planned.

CHAPTER 19

Tonga—We Gotta Be Bats

"Well, as they say, any landing you can walk away from is a good one," the flight attendant warbled over the PA System.

Drowsy from an arduous Trans-Pacific flight, Russ and I were snapped by to life by an abrupt jolt at Lupepau'u Airport. Although unaware of it at the time, this ill-fated awakening constituted a harbinger of things to come.

Our eye-drooping journey out of Portland, Oregon exceeded twenty-four hours. Crossing the International Date Line, we lost an entire day; it would be recovered two weeks later upon our return home.

From Portland we flew to Los Angeles, then onto Honolulu for a stopover. Tongatapa, which lay in the southern island group, would be our next stop. From there we flew to our final destination, for the first half of the trip, Vava'u, in the northern island group.

One of the few island monarchies left in the world, Tonga is organized into four main groups, spread over hundreds of miles in the South Pacific Ocean.

"What a spectacular place. It looks as though someone pasted the blue green spectrum on the globe." Enchanted by my aerial portal view, I couldn't wait to dive into the appealing sea.

After landing, we decided to take a catnap. Our short nap stretched, by accident, into several hours. After awakening, we arranged to go diving the next day. That could have proved a deadly decision.

In the ten years that I'd been diving, I'd logged hundreds of dives around the world, and never had a bad tank of air—never that is, until I dove on Vava'u.

A clear, sunny day awaited us. I bubbled with enthusiasm, thrilled at the opportunity to experience a virgin coral reef. The nearby site didn't take long to reach. Divers, one at a time, executed a backwards roll off the side of the boat.

I swallowed a large mouthful of salt water, not a pleasant experience. Russ, the dive master, and I waited for the other divers at the surface. After they joined us, each of us deflated our BC's; we were on our way down.

A powerful surge developed. It tossed us around like socks in a dryer. Not long after the descent, I began to feel ill. I attributed my malaise to the salt water I'd swallowed, and the conditions. I followed along with the group as they swam up and down through an underwater cave.

Generally, it's unwise for the person in charge to lead a dive with multiple depth changes. Some people have trouble equalizing the pressure in their ears, as I was. It can make for an uncomfortable, if not dangerous dive profile.

After weaving through the cave numerous times, we exited. I began to feel faint. I grabbed a coral head. *I might pass out*, I thought. I took a deep breath off my regulator; I realized the problem—bad air.

I could feel myself going limp, when a diver above me, by accident kicked off my mask. Water swirled in my face reviving me temporarily. I knew one thing. I had to get to the surface. I motioned to Russ, thumb up. He hurried over, knowing something was amiss. My buddy grabbed me and we kicked to the surface.

As soon as I could, I spit out my regulator and gasped for oxygen.

The boat driver, who was supposed to track the diver's bubbles, so he knew their location, wasn't anywhere near.

After what seemed like an eternity, the skipper spotted us and came to pick us up. As we bobbed in the rough ocean, I laid my head back and inhaled the fresh salty air. "Well, I guess any dive you can walk away from is a good one," I said.

Back on board, Russ took a whiff off my regulator.

"Gasoline."

Although we never discovered how the air became tainted, a fellow diver conjectured exhaust may have leaked off the gasoline-powered engine running the compressor.

The most disconcerting part of the disturbing incident occurred as we returned the tank. I informed the issuer of what had happened. "Smells a little funny," he said, and then wandered off.

"Humph." I couldn't believe his apparent lack of concern.

Russ canceled all further dives on Vava'u. I didn't even ask for a refund.

Although shaken by the experience, I still wanted to dive Tonga, but not there. At the end of the week, we'd be relocating to a different island group, Ha'apai.

Russ and I filled the remainder of our time on Vava'u snorkeling, browsing in the village, walking the island and sailing with Keith.

Keith, an entertaining New Zealander who moved to the islands about ten years ago, showed us around. His primary occupation consisted of taking tourists bill-fishing, but our visit fell during the off-season. He knew the waters well, and delivered us to white-sand beaches with offshore coral reefs to snorkel.

Early morning provided a pleasant time to walk, before the sun began its relentless pursuit. I'd set out for the market early and picked up fresh fruit—bananas, pineapples, mangos or coconuts. By late morning it became hot. The temperature lingered around ninety-eight degrees with ninety-eight percent humidity.

On a stroll at daybreak, I heard a rustle in the bushes. Three little pigs came tearing out of the jungle in front of us. Swine wandered the island. The pork-on-hoofs even roamed the beaches. It's amusing to see the porkers on the beach digging clams with their snouts, then hogging them down.

When rambling through the village, Russ noticed a playhouse-sized post office. Tonga promoted itself as "Being Where the New Day Begins." It occurred to us that some 2000 Millennium stamps might be of value, some day.

Two portly, perspiring Tongan women sat fanning themselves, looking fussed by the heat. The small postal structure had a couple of openings, but no breeze.

"Do you have any Tonga 2000 stamps?" I asked.

After sufficient deliberation, and a reluctant pause, one of them moved toward a grimy wood counter. She pulled out a worn, disarrayed, cardboard folder.

Placing it on the countertop, she began displayed the contents.

"The Millennium stamps. Cool!" I said, excited to have found them.

"We are too *hot*!" the postal worker said, after she narrowed her focus on me.

I forgot, although most Tongans speak English, they don't know American colloquialisms. Lesson learned.

With Keith's help, Russ and I entertained ourselves on Vava'u. However, both of us were looking forward to Ha'apai, and trying a dive there.

"Oh boy, now we get to go diving," I said, after switching islands.

We checked into the resort and inquired where to find the dive shop.

"I can tell you where the establishment is, but it won't do you any good," the hotel proprietor informed us, as he perused our registration forms.

"Why not?" I asked.

"The dive shop owner is on vacation."

"The dive shop owner is on vacation?"

"Uh, huh. Always go this time of year. Too dangerous to put the boat in the water."

I gazed out to sea from the outdoor lobby and observed water calm enough to fill a kiddy pool.

"Typically 90% of our hurricanes come through here the first week in March."

"Gee, it would have been nice if someone had told us."

"Yes. Someone should have told you."

Disappointment couldn't describe how we were feeling.

"We're here for a week," I said. "Guess we'd better try to make the best of it."

No car or scooter to rent; nowhere to go anyway. We walked the beach (often), snorkeled, and tried sea kayaking. I also attended a Tongan church ceremony.

Russ became obsessed with getting a photo of a bat. He spent a considerable amount of time in the pursuit of a flying fox. I became a little concerned when he began taking the camera on every outing. "Today might be the day," he said.

The Tongan church ceremony provided a definite highlight. Islanders, for the most part, are church-goers. It's frowned upon to do anything but attend service on Sunday. Children aren't supposed to play in the yard or swim in the sea. It is even illegal to drive, except when going to or from church.

We were invited to a Sunday gathering. I decided it would be interesting to go; Russ declined. I rode along with several inhabitants, and the resort's owner.

Everyone in the car spoke the native language. I felt a little awkward, as though I were eavesdropping, although I had no idea what the discussion entailed.

Women and children, walking roadside on the way to the church, paraded their Sunday finery. Little girls in white, frilly, organza dresses topped off by lacy hats with satin ribbons flowing, skipped along side their mothers, hand-in-hand.

As the parishioners filed in, and the pews filled, the choir sang—sang almost seemed like a euphemism. The rollicking hymns could have blown the roof off.

The entire service, delivered in Tongan, except for the last line: "Peace be with you." I hadn't understood the rest of it, but still found it to be uplifting. *Besides*, I thought, *I might know someone I should start praying for.*

The church ceremony provided me with a soaring spirit, while sea kayaking provided me with a swirling body. We'd never tried ocean-going rafting before.

"Let's give it a roll," I said to Russ.

"Are these hard to tip over?" I asked the rental attendant.

"No, they're easy to tip over," he said, laughed, then added in a serious manner, "They are very difficult to tip over."

As soon as he said that, I knew I would.

We dragged the kayaks across the beach, scampering to get off the hot sand and into the warm water. Russ and I made several unsuccessful attempts to launch. On our third try, we lurched from the beach.

Russ pointed his kayak toward a surrounding island. I'm not sure which one. I wasn't good at navigating. Wherever we ended up, was where we were.

"This is kinda tricky," I said as I tried to figure out how to use the paddle.

Finally my buddy and I were underway. After considerable effort, we inched forward a couple of feet. *Huh*, I thought, *this might be harder than it looks.*

After awhile, we were cruising. A distant island seemed to grow closer, but it proved to be an illusion.

"I think we're getting there." I hoped. We kept up our pathetic efforts until a shore lay a few hundred feet away.

Suddenly, a huge set of breakers arose, and headed straight toward us. *Huh-oh*, I thought, *what do we do now?*

"Go straight in. Don't get sideways," Russ said, as if reading my mind.

Wow, what a wild ride! Our strained efforts to make headway became history, as I was thrown forward, full throttle ahead. An enormous, final breaker pushed me to shore, but not before I executed a full roll.

"What a thrill!" I felt like a hotdog showing off, except I had no idea what I was doing. It occurred to me how exemplary of my approach this was. *I wouldn't want it any other way, it just wouldn't be as fun*, I thought.

Our last evening in Ha'apai, during our final bat walk, my buddy and I sauntered down the beach. I gazed up at the southern hemisphere constellations.

We stopped for a moment to admire the beauty and reflect on our journey, but only for a moment—because here came that bat again.

"I'm going to get him this time," Russ said.

We both knew it didn't matter. One thing our travels have taught us—life is about appreciating what we have. Bat picture or no bat picture.

The one that didn't get away—baby bat hanging out.
We finally got a picture.
Tonga

CHAPTER 20

Australia—Not the Greatest Barrier Reef

The Great Barrier Reef embodies a diver's ultimate dream destination. It's the largest single structure made by living organisms on earth. NASA's satellites monitor it from outer space. Six-hundred continental islands and three-hundred-fifty coral cays compose the behemoth. A gigantic coral reef, it sounded like a dream. We found instead that dreams don't always come true.

At a popular watering hole in Cairns, Australia, Russ and I shared a XXXX with a local diver, Downer. Russ asked him how the favored brew got its name, "Right, simple, mate. We can't spell beer," he replied with a twinkle in his eye.

After quaffing enough X's to win a game of tic-tac-toe, we engaged in a lively discussion of the best places in the world to dive. It seemed obvious he would argue the Great Barrier Reef. "Not so," our new buddy advised Russ, "I wouldn't spend my money divin' here, mate. The boats are too big and reefs have had too many anchors dropped on 'em." he urged us. "Go to Fiji."

Russ and I had learned leg-yanking constituted a favorite Aussie activity. We considered his advice and wondered if we had longer legs. He seemed sincere and passionate, but when leg-yanking takes the status of a national sport, like any professional athletes, they become good at it.

Russ and I had been to Tavenui, Fiji diving several times; we had to agree. It became one of our favorite places. The dive sites lingered a few minutes off shore; the reefs healthy, teeming with colorful life. Fiji offered spectacular diving. He gained credibility. My buddy and I further considered what we'd said.

We'd visited the Reef Fleet Terminal, where dive boats looked like cruise ships, far too large to proffer the intimate diving experiences we enjoyed. The closest dive sites lay an hour away. I tended to get seasick. Furthermore, rumors circulated of tiger sharks and box jellyfish.

One of the most lethal creatures known to mankind, this deadly species warrants serious avoidance. Downer launched on a tale about a dive mate that had been stung by a box jellyfish, "Came close to death, an excruciating one at that."

Toward the end of his story, I thought sightseeing might be a good idea.

Russ and I made only two dives; Hasting Reef, and Turtle Cove.

"Now we can say we made a couple of dives on the Great Barrier Reef," I said. Not much more to say. The dives lacked interest. Eighty people, mostly snorkelers, crowded the boat, with seven divers aboard. The descents featured seventy feet of visibility, little else.

"Saw several giant clams and a few sea anemones," Russ said as we climbed back aboard the boat.

"Trying to escape the guppies kicking at my mask was the most fun I had." Beginning snorkelers thrashed around on the surface.

Russ and I had to agree with Downer; Fiji yielded better diving. "Let's spend our time exploring the Cairns area," I said. "The guppy" ended our diving in Oz.

(Just as a note- conditions can change and numerous operators go to many different dive sites on the reef.)

Seeking adventure and excitement, we set out in search of the elusive platypus. This pint-size, furry, aquatic mammal with its comical bill, webbed feet, and broad flat tail, intrigued us. Its habitat is exclusively eastern Australia and Tasmania, so this trip afforded us a rare opportunity.

Russ rented a Nissan X-Trail from a local bloke. "You'll need a four-wheel drive for proper exploring," he advised, then added, "The road should be passable this time of year."

Headed north, toward Daintree National Park the lush vegetation thickened. Mossman town loomed in the distance as tropical rain forest enveloped us. The road went from paved, to gravel, to mud, over a dam, morphed into a stream, then into a river.

Russ pulled off the track by a small creek. Our map indicated, and a sign read, PLATYPUS VIEWING AREA. "This must be it," I said. A viewing blind sat adjacent to the parking area by a stream. We hid behind the blind and stayed quiet. Two hours later I said, "I think maybe we should employ a new strategy."

"I'll take you to that little place back there. You can ask how to find one."

We mud bogged into the scruffy town. He stopped at a mercantile; I went in.

"Excuse me, sir. How do you locate a platypus?" I inquired.

The Aussie gave me an odd look, trying to determine if I might have a few kangaroos loose in the top paddock, or was just a tourist. I must have appeared pathetic, he decided to help me.

"They are monotremes, the only egg-laying mammal," he said.

"Egg-laying mammal, that seems strange," I said.

"Absobloodylutely sport, they are related to—I kid ya," I thought he said.

This was a new development. Aussies liked to tease, but they didn't tell you when, I thought. I looked him right in the eye and said, "You're kidding me?"

"No," he said adding a chuckle. "Echidna, it's a spiny anteater."

I began to feel a bit discouraged, due to my failure to communicate and lack of platypus tracking abilities. I didn't give up easily, but made an exception.

"Ah, heck. Let's go to zoo. Maybe there's a platypus there."

Cairns Tropical Zoo is a small regional garden. Next to the box office sat a turnstile that meted people through one at a time. Once inside, visitors didn't have to find the animals, they found the visitors.

The ticket seller briefly described the facility, and mentioned, "You might be interested in our Cuddle a Koala Program." That grabbed my attention.

"Cuddle a koala?" I'd been infatuated with them since my honeymoon in Southern California. Years ago at the world famous San Diego Zoo, we stood in a zigzag line to enter the koala habitat, to view a barely visible bear at a distance.

Wanting nothing more that to get close to those adorable little creatures, perhaps hold one, I signed up. This dream came true.

Drowsing in eucalyptus trees, not three feet away, lazed a dozen koalas. Since they sleep eighteen hours a day, this wasn't surprising. Motionless lumps of fur appearing like teddy bears tossed on the branches, a few made slight movements or almost opened their eyes.

Snoopy, a male, yawned and reached for a eucalyptus leaf. I queued up to be first in line to cuddle him. I waited with great anticipation until the zookeeper bought him to me. I squealed with delight. If Snoopy was excited by all the attention, he didn't show it.

The diminutive critter reached out to me, grasping my upper arm. I pulled him close, feeling his soft furry body next to mine. Clinging to me, he conjured up thoughts of a warm puppy. He felt surprisingly light, males only weigh twenty pounds. I hugged him gently; he held on tightly. The brief encounter was over far too soon. I reluctantly returned Snoopy to his keeper. We continued on our way.

Touring the grounds, my buddy and I passed by an astounding array of animals including wallabies, wombats, crocodiles, tamarins, lemurs, dingoes and echidnas. Yes, echidnas but nary a platypus in sight.

Parrots: macaws, lorikeets, and lories dazzled us as we strolled through the aviary. "They look like rainbows in motion when they flutter their wings," I said.

Cassowaries, one of the largest living birds, had their own enclosure. Although shy, they can inflect serious injury if upset. Strange looking, they resemble an ostrich that escaped the pages of a kid's coloring book. Large three-toed feet, brightly colored heads on a black body and a spongy crest on their heads gave them a prehistoric, cartoon-like appearance.

Exploring the area around Cairns, we noticed numerous CASSOWARY CROSSING road signs. The Southern Cassowary—endangered in Queensland, seemed to hold a special place in the hearts of the Australians.

Kookaburras, though not as colorful, were a personal favorite. In grade school I remember singing about a kookaburra in a tree that ate gumdrops and cackled. What a great life, I thought. I later discovered I'd misheard the lyrics, he didn't eat gumdrops. Every morning we woke to his loud maniacal human-like laughter.

Now I know what he laughed about—waking everyone.

We lingered at the kangaroo enclosure. Sixty tame Eastern Grey kangaroos roamed freely. Hopping up and down, they looked like kernels in a popcorn popper. They leapt up to eat kangaroo chow from our hands. "They're real hum dingers, roo's are," an Aussie observed as he fed one, "Happy as a pig in mud."

Many of the female kangaroos had joeys. A sign by the enclosure admonished, DO NOT REMOVE JOEYS FROM POUCHES. Watching them jump around, I became curious, "Wonder why the youngsters don't go flying out?" We pondered that awhile, and then left noticing a little skip to our step.

On the way out we stopped at the concession stand for a final XXXX. "Cheers," my husband proposed, "Here's to Downer and the Land of Unders."

"I'll drink to that, X's and O's to you Oz; downright spiffy," I said.

The zoo's "Cuddle-a-Koala" Program, or Snoopy,
the koala's "Hug-a-Human" Program.
Cairns Tropical Zoo
North Queensland, Australia

Sue, wombat (rare Aussie burrowing marsupial), and zookeeper.
Cairns Tropical Zoo
North Queensland, Australia

Sue demonstrating an underwater signal, hi!
Great Barrier Reef, North Queensland, Australia

CHAPTER 21

Grenada—A Taste of Nice, Seafood and Spice

Violent winds howled, heavy rains fell and deadly waves came crashing ashore. In 2004, Hurricane Ivan destroyed ninety percent of Grenada's nutmeg crop, and wreaked havoc on cocoa plants. Sugarcane may have fared the best.

Hurricane Emily walloped Grenada again in 2005.

Greeting our, May 2010 arrival, fragrant aromas of the West Indies' Spice Isle floated through the cab's windows. Allspice, cinnamon, cloves, cocoa, mace, nutmeg and turmeric experienced rebirth on Grenada—one archipelago of the tri-island nation that also included Carriacou and Petite Martinique.

The taxi driver, at 2:00AM on the way to our hotel, belted out his country's National Anthem. "Welcome to my country," he said after finishing his serenade. "First time here?" He glanced in his rear-view mirror to watch our response.

"Yes, it is. Don't think I've ever been to a place that smelled so good." I tipped my head back and took a deep breath.

"You are special because you ride in my taxi. You are visitors now, but the next time you come, you will be family. If someone says you are not, you can take them to court and sue them." It seemed somewhat incongruent to receive such a warm welcome, an invitation to sue simultaneously. *Interesting place*, I thought.

The island offered a variety of activities. Russ and I toured gardens and farms, and pursued water-based activities—snorkeling and scuba diving.

Diving provided us with outstanding entertainment.

"Wanna lime?" Gary asked me one day after we'd finished diving. The twenty-something, good-looking dive master flashed a smile that could charm the fins off the fishes.

"No thanks. Do you have a cookie?'

"No." He chuckled. "Lime—that means hang out with your friends. Chill."

Chilling seemed like a good idea, since the temperature lingered around one-hundred degrees and the humidity tempted a thunderstorm. "Sure, why not?"

"When I took you in that air pocket, I thought our eyes were going to pop out of your head." Gary grabbed a drink and plopped down at the picnic table. He'd led me into the cramped chamber of the shipwreck *Veronica L.* Then he took his regulator out of his mouth and said, "Good morning."

"That did catch me by surprise. I'd never heard someone speak underwater. How did you do that?"

"Simple. When you weren't looking, I sneaked in and filled the chamber with air from my regulator. Then I came and got you."

"Tricky. But, why me?"

"Because, I thought you'd be the most fun."

I suppose I deserved it. When he banged on his tank to point out a puffer fish, I'd inflate my cheeks and form a circle with my arms. But that was because, when he pointed out a seahorse, he motioned riding a galloping bronco. I figured if he could ride, I could puff.

After diving on the *Veronica L.*, Gary said, "This is nothing. Wait until you see the *Bianca C.*" Legendary among divers it's known as

"The *Titanic* of the Caribbean."

The *Bianca C.*—a six-hundred-foot cruise ship—sunk after reaching St. George's Harbor in the '60's. An engine room explosion sparked an on-board fire. In an attempt to tow the blazing vessel beyond the harbor entrance and beach it, the tow rope broke. Having taken on too much water during towing, she sank to her final resting place, 130-feet down on the ocean's floor.

Our dive group performed a negative descent in the deep channel, necessary because of the depth we needed to attain quickly. The ship lay close to safe diving limits. The allotted bottom time wouldn't allow us to explore the entire length.

Poor visibility, fifty or sixty feet maximum, hindered our perspective. An obscured image of the wreck came into view. It sat upright on the bottom. We descended into the former swimming pool and made our way toward the bow.

Fish—mackerel, horse-eyed jacks, a pair of French angels and a spotted eel—swam in and around it. Sponges and black coral made themselves at home on the deck. Although massive, it didn't intrigue me the way the wrecks in the Truk Lagoon had. It lacked the artifacts that brought the other shipwrecks to life.

Shortly after we began to examine it, we received the signal to commence our gradual ascent. Each diver made the obligatory safety stop, and then surfaced.

"Well, now we can say we dove the *Bianca C.*," Russ said, as we bobbed in the water waiting for the boat to pick us up. "Too bad we didn't have more time."

The next outing, a case in point, demonstrated the fact that the real highlight wasn't always the diving, but sometimes rather the divers.

Purple Rain, the morning's dive site, featured an extensive healthy reef. The destination dazzled—but our dive buddies added the real pizzazz.

Joining on the boat were a couple of retired German gents, a set of twin sisters and a newlywed couple.

One of the older, affable fellows could have passed for Santa Claus. Good-natured, he would chuckle after everything he said—didn't matter whether it was funny or not. He had rosy red cheeks and a sunburned Rudolf-like nose. Sailing captured his heart. He appeared to merely be accompanying his diving friend.

Divers and Mr. Claus suited up, and rolled off the side of the boat, on the count of three. Part of Santa's suit, his weight belt, became dislodged; he lost a fin.

Gary hurried to his aid. He hefted the weight belt back up around the jolly fellow's waist and cinched it down. He then retrieved the fin which had floated off in the current.

"Gary's going to be busy today," Russ observed.

After Gary reassembled St. Nick's suit, we were ready to make our descent. Everyone deflated our B.C.'s and floated toward the bottom, except Mr. Claus.

He pranced about on the surface. Gary, once again to the rescue, grabbed Kris Cringle's deflator hose, held it above his head and slowly guided him down.

I sure hope he's better at going down chimneys. A lot of little kids would be awfully disappointed otherwise, I thought.

The dive proved rather unremarkable, with the exception of the seasonal fellow's buoyancy issues.

"How was the dive?" the skipper asked, as he helped us back up the ladder.

Father Christmas chuckled and said, "Well, I can tell you one thing—not all that coral is soft." We'd noticed he'd landed on it several times, bottom first. "And, I think, I may need to get a special weight belt attached by suspenders."

Red, no doubt.

The skipper returned to shore to exchange tanks. The short ride provided us a surface interval. As we waited for the new cylinders to be brought aboard, my buddy and I chatted with the twins.

They hailed from the University of Florida, Gainesville. One of them had won a contest that awarded her and a companion, free airfare. They used it to travel the Caribbean scuba diving.

"Enjoy your day" or "Enjoy the rest of your day" were often heard phrases around Grenada. The engaging sisters seemed to. Their impressions of the islands they'd visited proved informative; their stories quite entertaining.

The newlywed couple giggled, blushed and snuggled. They mostly kept to themselves. "That was us a few years ago," I said. A smile crept across my face.

We made two other dives: Kahonee and Molinere.

Kahonee—a mediocre dive with poor visibility—failed to awe.

Molinere housed contrived underwater sculptures. Sparse coral colonies, reef fish, sea fans and sponges existed in the surrounding Molinere Marine Reserve. The man-made structures appeared to have little, or no, impact on the sea life.

Overall, diving on Grenada just didn't seem that striking or spectacular.

"Did you go to Carriacou?" a fellow diver asked. Carriacou—we later discovered is known as the "Land of Reefs."

"No," I said. "We're only here for the week; took two days to get here."

"That's too bad. Diving and snorkeling there are great. Clear water. Beautiful reefs. Lots of fish. White Island is especially nice."

"Darn, I guess we'll have to come back." I thought about what our taxi driver told us, *If we come back, we'll be family.*

Although the diving wasn't the best we'd seen in the Caribbean, other positive experiences on the island compensated for it. Grand Anse, Morne Rouge Bay and Magazine Beach provided powdery, white-sand beaches fringed with palm and almond trees.

Grand Anse Beach, over two-miles long, and just to the south of St. George's, was the location of most hotels and resorts. The seashore's proximity to town made it an ideal place to hang out. Entrepreneurs must have concurred.

"See those buildings there?" a resident asked us, pointing out the strip of tourist facilities. "In 1997 there was nothing out there."

Morne Rouge Bay, behind our hotel, offered an unsurpassed place to get in the water. The high salinity, crystal-clear, warm water proved superb for floating or swimming.

Early morning provided a respite from the intense sun. Thunderstorms, just before daylight, alleviated the humidity and cooled the equatorial heat. A dawn swim became a favorite way to begin the day.

I felt the sand, already warm, work its way between my toes, as I waded out to the water. Balancing myself on one sunburned leg, resembling a pink flamingo, I pulled my fins on. Face down I glided away from the shore.

Eel grass flourished on the sandy bottom. Small bi-valves lay scattered about. Aquarium-size fish flittered in and out of the vegetation. The sun penetrated the shallow water, and cast rays of light to the bottom. A gentle current rippled the surface creating a sparkling cobweb effect.

I could have stayed there forever. However the local weatherman warned that a mere five minutes, at this latitude, during the hours from 10-4, constituted safe sun exposure. Despite the early hour, I'd already been in for thirty minutes.

I reluctantly kicked back to shore. *This is one of the best places in the world to swim*, I thought as sat in the sand taking my fins off.

Sur La Mer Restaurant sat on the back of the beach, nestled among the trees. It offered a wide selection of international and Caribbean cuisine, with emphasis on fresh seafood.

That evening Russ and I returned. We dined under a huge palm frond that swayed above a candlelit table. I slipped off my sandals. Cockeyed in our chairs, as the sand shifted underneath their legs, we gazed out upon the water.

Moonlight danced on the shore. Glancing up toward the beam's origin, I noticed that magnificent homes sat atop the surrounding bougainvillea draped cliffs. "Could you imagine owning one of those? Life would be a beach," I said.

A genial waitress interrupted my enchantment. "Good evening," she said, as she handed us the over-sized menus. "How was your day?"

"It couldn't have been better. Thank you," I said.

A long-legged, white wading bird strutted by our table, temporarily distracting me. I refocused my attention on the menu, but what I really needed to know was what Russ intended to order.

"What are you having Russ?" I pretended to look at the specials board.

"Lobster sounds good."

"I'm sorry sir. Lobster is out-of-season," the waitress said.

"Well then, I'll take the Flaming Caribbean Rum Shrimp and Stuffed Crab Back." He knew I wanted his food, so once in awhile he ordered for both of us. That way, when I traded with him, he'd still have something he liked.

The food proved so delicious, we thought we'd try to find the Aquarium Restaurant on Magazine Beach. Our singing taxi driver had recommended it. He'd said, "It's a can't miss."

"I think we missed it," I said. Surprisingly, after driving around most of the island, Russ discovered it behind the airport. I wouldn't have looked there.

A wooden deck extended out from the restaurant, over the beach. The back of the eatery abutted a sea-cliff giving it a cool, cavernous effect. A huge fish tank sat off to one side, rife with tropical fish.

Wait-staff hurried around long tables, their chairs tied with organza bows. "We're getting ready for a wedding reception. Please make yourselves at home. We'll open at noon for lunch," one of the congenial waitresses informed us.

After walking on the beach, we returned to a table on the deck. As we sat watching the waves, an older English gentleman, fins and snorkel in hand, sat down at the table next to us. "Beautiful day, heh?" he said.

"Yes, a beautiful day in a beautiful place. Lovely restaurant," I said.

"Glad you like it. My daughter owns it," he said. "I'm waiting for my grandchildren."

We chatted until his grandchildren arrived with a brand-new, lovable, five-week old black Rottweiler puppy in tow.

"I want to be a veterinarian," his granddaughter said as she passed me the adorable pup. "I have to go off-island for my basic education, but I can return here to go to vet school."

St. George's University, founded thirty years ago as a Caribbean medical school, grew. It now includes a veterinary school among other programs.

The grandkids wandered off with the puppy as we continued our chat. "I was stationed here after the Grenada invasion in 1983," he said. "Of course, I'm retired now." He spent the next hour entertaining us with nautical tales from his years in the British Navy.

As it turns out, he was why lobster wasn't on the menu. He'd been farsighted enough to realize, that continued overfishing of the crustaceans, would eventually lead to their demise. "The locals hated me," he said. "They'd point at me and say, "There's that white guy who said we couldn't fish lobster." He stopped for a minute and stared out to the sea. His thoughts seemed far away.

"I'll go get a menu. You lovely people have waited long enough for lunch," he said as he got up. He returned with the menus; we made our selections.

After we ordered fresh, in-season seafood and ice teas, he said, "Let me share a recipe with you for the best ice tea on earth. Take a few Earl Grey teabags, boil them proper and add some nutmeg syrup. Place the whole bloody lot in the refrigerator for twelve hours, then enjoy."

Nutmeg syrup was a local specialty. Next on our agenda were the farm tours. The nutmeg station was one of our first stops. I picked up a bottle of sirop de muscade (nutmeg syrup) and gave his recipe a go. It tantalized the taste buds—sweet and spicy—a refreshing treat for a hot summer day.

Driving around the island proved challenging. Russ learned to stay out of St. George. The capital presented special difficulties. Two-way streets turned into one-way streets without warning. The traffic sped along, beyond what was reasonable or safe.

Townspeople crowded the cramped spaces. They darted in and out of shops, and then stopped in the road for quick chats. Bedlam intensified when tourists flooded off the cruise ships.

Random traffic circles popped up, as did stoplights in the most unexpected places. Once in town, we felt as though we were trapped in a maze, and couldn't get out. After several attempts, Russ hit upon the right combination of one-way streets and traffic circles to escape.

We headed up the coast, feeling more lucky than clever, to have engineered our getaway. "It should get easier now," I said. I've always been somewhat stupidly optimistic. Driving the island presented new formidable challenges.

Mini-buses provided the main source of transport around the island. The owners' logos and/or mottos, or their route number and destination, were emblazoned across the tops of the front windshields.

No pullouts existed. When someone wanted off, the driver stopped—in the middle of the narrow, twisting road. This necessitated swerving into the on-coming lane of traffic, or getting rear-ended.

With a little luck, we reached the Belmont Estates. Brent, the operations manager, welcomed us and gave us a personal tour. The agri-tourism attraction grew nutmeg and cocoa. "Bet you don't know where mace comes from."

"Probably from the mace plant," I said.

"Nope. Mace is the covering of the nutmeg; had no idea till I started working here." He meant the historic estate that dated back to the late 1600's. Originally the old plantation grew coffee and sugar.

He explained cocoa processing. The cacao bean supplies three products: chocolate liquor, cocoa butter and cocoa powder.

"The ladies 'walked the beans.' They used their feet to turn them over, so they could dry. Because of the cocoa butter they had extremely soft feet." He showed us the huge trays of beans that lay on moveable racks. "If we get a thunderstorm, the call goes out, 'Rain down,' and everyone drops what they're doing and hustles over to push the trays into the shelter."

"So the beans have to dry out to make the cocoa?" I thought I noticed a trend.

"Yes. They started out as 'wet cocoa'—buckets of cocoa seeds that had been taken from ripe cocoa pods. When the seeds are removed from the pods, they're covered in a thick white pulp. The kids love them—taste like litchis."

After the tour, Brent made us some cocoa tea—a delicious, rich concoction made by dropping preformed balls into boiling water and whole milk. "These are available for sale, along with Grenada Chocolate Company bars, in our gift shop."

"And, where might that be?" I tried to decide how many cases I wanted. As I sipped the steaming drink, I realized how hot it was. "But won't they melt?"

"Just avoid milk chocolate. It's the milk that makes it melt, not the cocoa."

"Interesting, I didn't know that about chocolate." I sampled one of the 71% cocoa bars.

Chocolate, it seems is available in different forms: Unsweetened—pure chocolate liquor (baking chocolate); dark or plain—semi-sweet and bittersweet; and milk—solid with milk in some form; cocoa powder; and compound chocolate—confection of cocoa and vegetable fat. White chocolate really isn't chocolate, but a confection of nutmeg, sugar and fat.

"You know what?" I lifted the bar to my mouth.

"No, what," Russ said munching on a 60% cocoa bar.

"This smells like feet."

"You're just imaging it because Brent told us how they turn the beans."

"I guess so." I took a nibble. "May smell like feet, but it sure tastes good."

After finishing our snack, we gathered our courage and hit the road to the River Antoine Rum Distillery.

Russ and I were greeted by personable Whitfield Lyons who showed us around. The manufacturing plant constructed in 1785, made it possibly the oldest distillery in the Caribbean.

Water from a nearby river powered the huge ancient waterwheel. The wheel turned the gigantic crusher, which extracted juice from sugar cane. The juice was then sent through a series of copper bowls heated by fire. From there it went into cooling tanks, where fermentation began. In the last step, it was re-heated and then distilled.

"We make regular rum and spiced rum punch," Whitfield said as he offered us a sample.

I tried the regular rum. "Whoa, that's potent stuff." It burned all the way down.

"You might prefer the rum punch; it's not quite so strong."

"I think I'll pass. Thanks though." I recalled Litl' Punch's big wallop on Martinique. I didn't want to get smacked again.

Tomorrow would be our last day. "Let's go to Annandale Falls," I suggested.

"We can do that, maybe."

On the way to the falls we took the wrong road(s) and ended up on the other side of the island. My philosophy is, "You're never lost; you just don't always know where you are." We found ourselves at La

Sagesse Bay at lunchtime.

La Sagesse, another horseshoe-shaped bay with sparkling-clean, turquoise water. The open-air restaurant, sat on perfectly manicured grounds, and offered a superb ocean view. Russ ordered Conch in Creole Sauce and Shrimp in Garlic Sauce. I enjoyed both of them.

We crossed the island, and headed for the interior. The falls were located below Grand Etang National Park. Close to the southwest peninsula—near many of the visitors' facilities—they were popular with tourists.

We happened to arrive the day the mini-buses arrived with cruise ship passengers. Apparently local vendors ramped up their efforts for them. The parking lot bulged with island transport vehicles and roadside vendors.

"Come have your picture taken with the banana women," the merchant wielding his camera offered. The women twirled about in bold, sherbet-color plaid, ankle-grazing skirts; overlaying white eyelet petticoats. Atop their heads sat baskets of tropical fruit, including bunches of bananas. Gold hoop earrings, the size of saucers, dangled from their ears.

As I admired their balancing abilities, I felt something touch my arm. I spun around to see a mona monkey, held by his owner, reaching out to me.

"Picture with the monkey?" the roadside entrepreneur asked.

I considered my options. I could have my picture taken with the banana women, a mona monkey or Russ. I opted for Russ.

My buddy and I jockeyed our way out of the jam-packed parking lot. We'd made progress in navigating Grenada—learned a few landmarks along the way. Now it was time to go home.

"Well, what did you think of our trip to 'Spice Paradise'?" Russ asked, as he backed the rental into our assigned parking spot one last time.

"I'd say, like all our vacations, it was nothing to sneeze at. Spice, pepper—get it?"

Sunset shot on the dock at St. George.
Grenada

CHAPTER 22

Adventures and Antics—Escapades

Our diving experiences etched vivid, lifelong impressions. One rainy afternoon, in a sentimental mood, I started flipping through a photo album. Memories spilled out; my buddy and I revisited a few.

1989. A shot of me holding the oyster, trying to muster the courage to swallow it. "That's where our journey began."

I turned the page. "Cozumel, first international flight; never left the country without a dental exam after that."

"Aah, look, Toothy." A wave of nostalgia swept over me. The dive club's October activity required carving a pumpkin underwater. "Nobody wanted to do it but me. I said, 'I'm going to find someone like me.' Remember what you said?"

"There isn't anybody else like you."

"That's right. But I talked Mary into it. She tossed Toothy down, then joined me. I began carving, the lid floated off. Tried again, succeeded. Never gave up."

I advanced another page as I continued to muse.

A guy grinned. He held up two gigantic lobsters, one in each hand. "There's Rich with the contraband crustaceans he smuggled into

Merrill Lake's crawdad dive." The Bottom Timers Dive Club held an annual contest to bag the biggest crawfish at the freshwater lake.

"I remember. He hid them in his BC—one in each pocket—descended, took them out, stuck 'em in his goody bag, then surfaced."

"He bagged a couple of whoppers. Everyone had a good laugh."

We continued perusing. "Oh, no." I'd tried to forget the Fin Flopper Award, but the photographic evidence stared at me. I stood red-faced, shaking hands with the dive club's president, accepting the dubious accolade. My nomination, Bottoms Up Bottom Timer took the trophy. "Geez, I just knew that darn Campbell River dry suit incident might push me over the top."

"Yeah." Russ laughed. "Nobody else even got a vote, did they?"

"I don't remember."

"Oh, look at this. *Ah Baloney* in shallow water at Freshwater Bay, still on the trailer. Do you recall that?" Now it was my turn.

"No."

"I do. You accelerated, and then jammed on the brakes, to try and jerk the boat off the trailer." I started laughing. "But you forgot to remove the tie-downs. How many times did you lurch that poor Chevy forward?"

"I don't remember."

"Look, *Escape*." A myriad of memories floated around our sleep aboard boat.

"The antennas are up." I knew Russ wouldn't forget the trip he neglected to put them down. "Reminds me of the time we left the boat bumpers out, and cruised down I-5 South with them flapping and banging." I stopped to ponder for a moment. "I think I figured out why you decided to sell it."

"We weren't using it anymore."

"Yeah, because every time we did, something embarrassing happened."

I figured I'd better turn the page, or our trip down memory lane could reach a sudden dead end.

I stopped at a photo taken at Battle Rock Motel, Port Orford, Oregon. "Lucy and Ounce." The diving wasn't memorable, but Lucy—a huge, long-hair cat and her buddy, Ounce—a tiny, nervous little dog, captivated me. "It's sure odd the things I recollect."

I skipped a few pages, and landed on a snapshot taken at Mulege. "*Senor* Webb, he is standing in front of Mexican village oasis' hardware store."(*sic*)

I recalled sauntering into the dimly lit *tienda*. The proprietor greeted us. We'd planned a picnic at Isla El Requesion—had a can of SPAM, chips, a couple of Coronas, but no bread. I asked where it might be.

He looked at me, like I'd made one too many dives, and replied in broken English, "You get bread at *panaderia*, bakery."

I continued rifling through the memories. "Hippopotamuses, I thought I'd die laughing. Those two eighty-year-old ladies were great. You and I had missed our Cook Island's connecting flight, so we drove to San Diego. Went to the Zoo, and I spied the hippos."

"You laughed, forgot what tickled you, and then made that funny sound."

"'Did that thing snort?' the lady asked her friend. They thought the 'potamus made the noise—an absolute riot."

"Look at that face." Russ said, after he'd flipped the page.

"I'd tasted the Aussie's brown yeast paste for the first time. Never tasted anything quite like that before."

"Look at this. I forgot I stuck it in here. It's my letter from Portland's KGW former radio personality, Craig Walker."

"He selected your 'Stump the Jock' question to go into the hundred year time capsule, announced it as we carpooled to work. I remember how excited you got."

"Well, I figured it was one way of going down in history."

"I forgot the question."

"The contest entailed figuring out something representative of current times. My question—'What is America's favorite snack food?'"

"Well?"

"I'm not going to tell you." I reconsidered. "Maybe later, I'll give you a little food for thought."

"What else have we here?" I continued browsing. "We had so much fun."

"It's been an interesting twenty years."

"I'm going to grab another album. How many do we have anyway?"

"Well, let's see. Land photos we have about a dozen, then I started storing them in the computer, and only printing out our favorites. Underwater shots." Russ stopped to think for a moment. "Um, I'd say one or two—albums."

I opened up the archive to a photograph of Colours of the Sea—our 1991 showcase exhibit at Oregon Museum of Science and Industry (OMSI) in Portland. Russ and I were members of the Oregon Society of Conchologists; they held an annual shell show. "Remember our premise?"

"That cold water species are usually dull in color. I even recall our conclusion; that light, temperature and diet may all affect shell color." Russ had an amazing memory.

"As usual, while I stood on my head, you put yours to work. We won the Dupont Trophy. I should say, you won…"

"It was teamwork, you hand-lettered the display."

"Yeah, my spelling of 'colors' may have influenced the judges. It seemed classy, sort of professor-like." Russ sat staring at me. At times, he couldn't believe what I dreamt up.

I skipped through several more pages. Sumesi, our friend's Fijian boatman ferried us from Tavenui to a nearby atoll. "Spray hit him in the face, so he grabbed his mask—snorkel attached, and put it on.

Clever of him; it seemed to work," Russ commented.

"Cook Islands, Tangaroa. That big boy impressed me."

DUH. White coral pieces lay roadside, arranged on black smooth lava, approaching the Kona airport. "I talked you into stopping and adding to the clever graffiti. I thought maybe you'd add, Russ + Sue, or maybe Russ loves Sue, but you spelled out, 'duh.'"

"Only one there."

"You and I had such wonderful times in Hawaii. I figured we made fourteen trips to the islands. For awhile we went every year. Remember Dick of Kailua-Kona, the guy that sold Christmas decorations in the South Pacific? That's what I call a salesman. And, Rocky of Hilo, and Reggie of Oahu's Bishop Museum, and the Kona Coast Divers crew. Such nice people." I couldn't remember them all.

"I'll never forget our first trip there, our honeymoon. The flight turned out to be a rooter's bus for the Oregon Ducks." I could still recall the excitement. "We weren't even certified divers then. Maui's Molokini Crater snorkeling trip may have been what hooked us."

"You might be right."

It represented an extra-special memory. The thrill of being in warm open water, surrounded by coral and fish, felt amazing.

"Tiger shark." I needed to say no more. I sat on the beach smiling, next to a sand sculpture of a shark. I felt happy to be alive.

Twenty years after we received our scuba certification, Russ and I found ourselves in the water, being circled by a twelve-foot tiger shark in Honokohau Harbor off Kona.

Dolphins and their calves that frolicked in the water near us disappeared. I glimpsed something above. In near shock, I watched the huge, frightening predator glide around us in a slow circle. Adrenalin powered, I kicked like my life depended on it—and it may have—over to Russ. I grabbed his arm, hyperventilating. A passel of bubbles filled the ocean. I motioned up.

"I'll never forget that look on your face. I thought your eyes were going to pop out of your mask."

"I have to admit, I'd never been so terrified. You pulled me down to the bottom and we furiously kicked to get back to the shore—that's all I recall. All these years, I never knew you could swim faster than me."

"You know the old joke. You don't have to swim fast, you just have to swim faster..."

"Yeah, yeah. Whether you admit it or not, you were scared too. I've never seen you move that fast."

"After diving for many years, I guess we'd have to consider that our grand finale."

"I guess so. All I know is I'd never care for an encore. Doritos."

"Doritos?" He looked at me quizzically.

"Those were America's favorite snack food. I said I'd tell you later. I'm gonna tell the shark too. Maybe he'll find them tastier than divers."

Sue and her nemesis (luckily, only a land sand shark).
Kailua-Kona, Hawaii

EPILOGUE

My Renaissance man has developed new interests. He now repairs and restores antique radios, primarily from the Art Deco period. He battles poison oak, buckbrush and wildfires on our tree farm in Southern Oregon. He continues to work as a senior cellular technician.

Occasionally, he'll get out his Lemon Twist Yellow, 1970 Plymouth 'Cuda. After he's brushed the dust off the hood, we'll take it for a spin. It's the same one he wooed me in so long ago.

I bake blackberry pies, pull weeds, water plants and chase my kitties around. Sporting oversized shades, I zip around town in a fast, electric-blue, tuner car. Inside I'm twenty-five again. Jimmy Buffet ballads blast out the sunroof. All the windows are down and my hair is blowing in the breeze. The kids stare and gape as if they're wondering, "What's she doing driving *that*?" I'm having fun.

Russ and I still go diving, but we don't "dive our brains out" anymore. We get out the old photo albums and wonder where the years have gone. Once, we'd stopped at a picture of me swallowing the oyster at scuba certification, I'd said, "Geez, I looked *so* young."

"Hard to believe that picture was taken twenty years ago," Russ had said.

A sense of tremendous gratitude befell me. I realized I'd been fortunate enough to live my dreams and share them with my buddy.

The adventure continues.

CPSIA information can be obtained at www.ICGtesting.com
Printed in the USA
LVOW06*1952191213

366070LV00013B/1043/P